The DENVER CHRONICLE

From A Golden Past

The DENVER CHRONICLE

From A Golden Past To A Mile-High Future

David Kent Ballast

Gulf Publishing Company

Thank you, Anna.

The Denver Chronicle
From a Golden Past to a Mile-High Future

Copyright © 1995 by Gulf Publishing Company, Houston, Texas. All rights reserved. Printed in the United States of America. This book, or parts thereof, may not be reproduced in any form without permission of the publisher.

All photographs by author unless otherwise stated.

Gulf Publishing Company
Book Division
P.O. Box 2608 □ Houston, Texas 77252-2608

10 9 8 7 6 5 4 3 2 1

Library of Congress Cataloging-in-Publication Data

Ballast, David.
    The Denver chronicle : from a golden past to a mile-high future / David Ballast.
        p.   cm.
    Includes bibliographical references (p.) and index.
    ISBN 0-88415-202-2 (hbk). — ISBN 0-88415-201-4 (pbk)
    1. Denver (Colo.)—History. I. Title.
F784.D457B35   1995
978.8'83—dc20   94-24411
                                                 CIP

Contents

Acknowledgments ix

Foreword xi

Introduction xiii

PART ONE **Boom Town on the Prairie
1858 to 1892** 1

    Gold in Colorado Territory   1

    Building a Prairie Town   8

    Transportation at the Crossroads
      of the West   30

    Education and the Arts in Early Denver   39

    Early Denver Politics   47

PART TWO   **The City Beautiful
                    1893 to 1930** **53**

   Mayor Speer and the City Beautiful   54
   Growth After the 1893 Depression   64
   The Expanding City   81
   The Ku Klux Klan in Colorado   108

PART THREE   **From Bad Times to Recovery
                    1930 to 1945** **110**

   City and County Building
      Construction   112
   Surviving the Depression   116
   The New Deal for Denver   119
   Denver During World War II   128

PART FOUR   **Growth After World War II
                    1946 to 1973** **133**

   The Post-World War II Boom   134
   Denver's New Building Boom   139
   Transportation Changes   155
   Suburban Growth   161
   Cultural and Educational
      Development   164

PART FIVE   **21st-Century Boom Town**
               1974 to the present **171**

   Growth in the '70s and '80s   172
   Building for the Common Good   180
   Economic Boom and Bust   188
   Cultural and Educational Expansion   191

Sports Mania **195**
Sources **198**
Index **200**

Acknowledgments

I would like to first thank Curtis Casewit, who got me started on this project, and Thomas J. Noel for his advice and reading of the manuscript. Special thanks to Eleanor Gehres and the staff at the Denver Public Library's Western History Department and to those at the Colorado State Historical Society library.

For helping me compile many of the historic photographs, a "thank you" to Mary Miller at Elitch Gardens, Doris Payne at Gates Rubber Company, Jim Saccamano with the Denver Broncos Football Club, Julie Roberts at the Colorado Convention Center, and Ken Fuller, Architect.

Additional photographs were provided by Emmett Jordan with Rich Clarkson and Associates, Philip B. Demosthenes at the Colorado Department of Transportation, Al Green with the General Services Administration, Kevin Graham at Public Service Company of Colorado, and Jeffrey R. Krump with Denver's Division of Theaters and Arenas.

More photographs were loaned to me by Elaine Gleason at First Interstate Bank of Denver, Cynthia Nakamura and the Denver Art Museum, Sandy Chotechuang at Denver Water, Jim Parker in the Research Division of the Colorado State Archives, Evan McCollum at Martin Marietta Astronautics, Carol De Armont at the Regional Transportation District, Sandy Lasky with the Colorado Symphony, Bonnie McCune at the Denver Public Library, Steve Klodt and the Denver International Airport Public Affairs Office, and Mike Levy and Virginia Steel with the Wings Over the Rockies Aviation and Space Museum.

Foreword

David Ballast, a lifelong resident of the Mile-High City, has watched Denver evolve into a high-rise giant during the past half century. Dave was born into a quiet town of brick and stone buildings dating to the gold and silver booms of the 19th century that bears little resemblance to today's metropolis of some two million people.

The Ballast family is legendary, especially in North Denver, where Dave's father, Louis Ballast, operated one of Denver's first drive-in restaurants. At the Humpty Dumpty on Speer Boulevard, Louis in 1935 developed—and applied for a trademark on—the world's first cheeseburger.

You will find more than cheeseburgers in the following pages. David is an architect and the author of two fine previous works on Denver's celebrated Civic Center Park and on the Denver Art Museum.

Savor this introduction to Denver. It captures the history and flavor of one of America's most livable cities—and a terrific town for tourists.

Thomas J. Noel

Tom Noel is a columnist for *The Denver Post*, a Denver Landmark Preservation Commissioner, chair and professor of history at the University of Colorado at Denver, and the author of numerous books on Denver and Colorado.

Introduction

Denver is a city that probably shouldn't have happened. It was isolated on the high plains in Indian territory hundreds of miles from civilization. It wasn't near any navigable waterways. It was arid and nearly treeless. Even the gold that brought the first prospectors to the confluence of Cherry Creek and the South Platte River never really amounted to anything—the riches were in the mountains.

But people came anyway, lured by the opportunity and the beauty of the region. The pioneers made a home. They found water, built railroads, and planted trees.

Denver prospered from the gold and silver found in the mountains and from the crops and livestock raised on the plains. The city grew with transportation, warehousing, and tourism. Manufacturing, military installations, and federal government offices attracted more people. Most recently, oil, gas, and high technology have fueled the prosperity of the metropolitan area.

Early Denverites wanted to make the city great; today's citizens still have that spirit. The recent rapid growth of the front range is challenging Denver as never before. Still, with all the problems facing us, Denverites enjoy a prosperous economy, a relaxed lifestyle, recreational opportunities, cultural amenities, a near-perfect climate, sunshine, and brilliant blue skies. There is something good here. I'm glad it did happen.

David Ballast

PART ONE

Boom Town on the Prairie

Gold in Colorado Territory

Today, tourists stroll in and out of the shops along Larimer Square. Locals sip gourmet coffee in the warm morning sunlight. Above the shops, business people begin another day of seeking their fortunes or simply working in a city they love. A few hundred feet toward the snow-capped mountains, Cherry Creek gently flows northwest where it drains into the South Platte River about three-quarters of a mile away. Another day begins along Larimer Street. "Larimer Street at present is the best, Lawrence and McGaa next," wrote General William Larimer to his wife on November 30, 1858. (McGaa is now Market Street.)

Larimer was writing to his wife shortly after he and his gold prospecting party had formed the Denver City Town Company east of Cherry Creek, not far from where it joins the South Platte River. But the General was not the first to seek his fortune at the foot of the Rocky Mountains. As early as the 16th century, Spanish explorers led by Francisco Vásquez de Coronado explored in New Mexico and Kansas looking for the elusive metal. In 1850, Lewis Ralston discovered gold in Ralston Creek (a tributary of Clear Creek) in Arvada while he was leading a

1

1) *General William Larimer, Jr., traveled from Leavenworth, Kansas, to the Pikes Peak Region after hearing of gold discoveries. On November 17, 1858, he crossed Cherry Creek from Auraria, jumped a prior claim, and five days later established the Denver City Town Company. (Courtesy, Colorado Historical Society)*

group of prospectors to the newly discovered California gold fields. The yield from the creek was small compared to what was waiting in California, so they moved on after making a note in their diaries.

For many years after the Ralston discovery the area remained inhabited, as it had always been, by native American Indians, only occasionally visited by explorers and fur trappers. Several tribes had inhabited eastern Colorado during the past 1,000 years. The Cheyenne and Arapaho occupied northeastern Colorado at about the same time the area was purchased from France in 1803 as part of the Louisiana Purchase. Later, the remainder of what was to become Colorado was taken from Mexico in 1848 after the Mexican War.

Because the United States wanted to ensure the safety of the pioneers and prospectors traveling to California, the government began to negotiate treaties with the Indians. One of the most significant was the Treaty of Fort Laramie, which divided up the newly acquired land among the various tribes. The United States gave the Arapahos and Southern Cheyennes the land between the Arkansas and North Platte Rivers from the base of the mountains to a line about 200 miles east. Ten years later, the government recognized it needed legal ownership of the newly settled area, including Denver City. The United States negotiated the Treaty of

2) Before Denver was founded, the Cheyenne and Arapaho Indian tribes occupied northeastern Colorado. The Closing Era statue on the east lawn of the Capitol grounds represents the passing of two original inhabitants of the region, the Indian and the bison, as the settlers came to Colorado. The sculpture, by Preston Powers, was displayed at the Columbian Exposition in Chicago in 1893 before being placed near the Capitol.

Fort Wise with the Arapahos and Cheyennes, which was signed on February 18, 1861. Although the validity of the treaty is still debated, it legalized possession of the region, including Denver, by the United States. Ten days later Congress designated the area Colorado territory, naming it after the Colorado River.

While ownership was changing in the Rocky Mountain region in the first part of the 19th century, William Larimer was developing his taste for real estate development. Born in 1809 in Pennsylvania, Larimer ran a freight service in the early 1830s, helped organize the Westmoreland Coal Company, ran a wholesale grocery and produce business, and managed a hotel owned by his father. He was in the military as early as 1828 and was named Major General of the Pennsylvania State Militia in 1852. He became a banker and the first President of the Pittsburgh & Connellsville Railroad, during which time he invested in various companies including California gold mining enterprises and overland transportation companies. General Larimer formed the La Platte and Larimer City Town Companies in Nebraska in 1855, where he was also a member of the state legislature for two years. His interest in Colorado gold was sparked by news from other prospectors and fortune-seekers like himself.

One of those prospectors was a Georgia farmer named William Green Russell. Russell had tried digging for gold in his home state, but when he heard of the gold discovery on Ralston Creek he decided to strike it rich in the Pikes Peak region. He joined other groups and some relatives and set out for Colorado in February 1858.

Russell and his gold expedition of more than 100 people arrived at the junction of Cherry Creek and the South Platte River in late June 1858. They had little luck finding any gold, and many decided to return home. Russell and a few others stayed and camped near Little Dry Creek, a trickle of water flowing into the Platte River. By today's bearings, it was about at West Dartmouth and Santa Fe Drive.

Here they found gold in paying quantities. It was soon depleted and the prospectors grew tired of the camp, moving north to Wyoming in search of higher-yielding rivers. In the fall they returned to the mouth of Cherry Creek to establish winter quarters, setting up a permanent settlement on the west side of Cherry Creek near the Platte River. Joined by other prospectors in the area, William Green Russell and his brothers formed the town of Auraria on November 1, 1858, naming it after their hometown in Georgia.

3) *This sketch shows how the first settlement near the junction of the South Platte River and Cherry Creek might have looked in 1859 with Pikes Peak in the distance on the left. The town was called Auraria and was founded on November 1, 1858, by William Green Russell, a prospector from Georgia. Cherry Creek is visible in the foreground. (The Denver Public Library, Western History Department)*

Across the creek, some of the former members of a party from Lawrence, Kansas, had settled. Earlier, the Lawrence party had prospected along the South Platte and had established a ragtag collection of cabins in what they called Montana City, north of Russell's original find at Little Dry Creek. They soon abandoned Montana City and traveled farther north to the mouth of Cherry Creek with the express purpose of establishing a town there and exploiting it.

They met two Indian traders, John Smith and William McGaa, who claimed they had control of the land because they were married to Indian wives. With cooperation from the Indians and somewhat dubious title to the land through Smith and McGaa, the group formed the St. Charles Town Company in September 1858 and staked out an area one mile square on the east side of Cherry Creek.

After organizing the settlement, the St. Charles people returned east to charter their new town and avoid winter on the high plains. On the way east they passed another party headed west, which made them consider the safety of their claim. One of the members, Charles Nichols, was sent back to erect a building and protect the claim until the rest of the group returned in the spring.

At the time, William Larimer was in Leavenworth, Kansas, where his brother, John McMasters Larimer, was working in a bank. One day a man brought in a goose-quill inkwell filled with flakes of what he believed was gold and wanted it analyzed. John Larimer made the verification. The man was from the group camped on the banks of Cherry Creek and the Platte River.

When the General heard of this, he promptly organized an expedition. There were only six people in his original party, but they were later joined by others on their way to gold country. One of the six included Larimer's son, William H. H. Larimer, then only 18, who later recalled preparations for their trek across the wilderness: "The first thing we put into the bottom of our wagon was six light pine boards. We did not know just what we might want to use them for, but a fellow who was standing close by when we were loading them on the wagon remarked that they would be used for coffins." Undaunted by the dangers, the Larimer party set out from Leavenworth on October 1, 1858. Traveling about 20 miles a day along the southern route to the Pikes Peak region, they arrived at the mouth of Cherry Creek on November 16, 1858.

In the meantime, Charles Nichols had barely laid in a few logs of his cabin to claim the site on the east bank of Cherry Creek as the city of St. Charles. The original six members of the Larimer party first camped on the west side of Cherry Creek, in Auraria. However, Larimer believed the east side of the creek was better suited for a town, no doubt recognizing the obvious fact that the Auraria site had already been claimed a few weeks earlier. He crossed the river and placed four cottonwood poles which he called the foundation of his settlement and claimed the site for a town on Wednesday, November 17, 1858.

Larimer maintained that there was no evidence of a prior claim. He obviously overlooked the survey stakes of the St. Charles group and did not recognize the validity of the unfinished cabin on the site as staking any kind of claim or proving that anyone was there before him. William

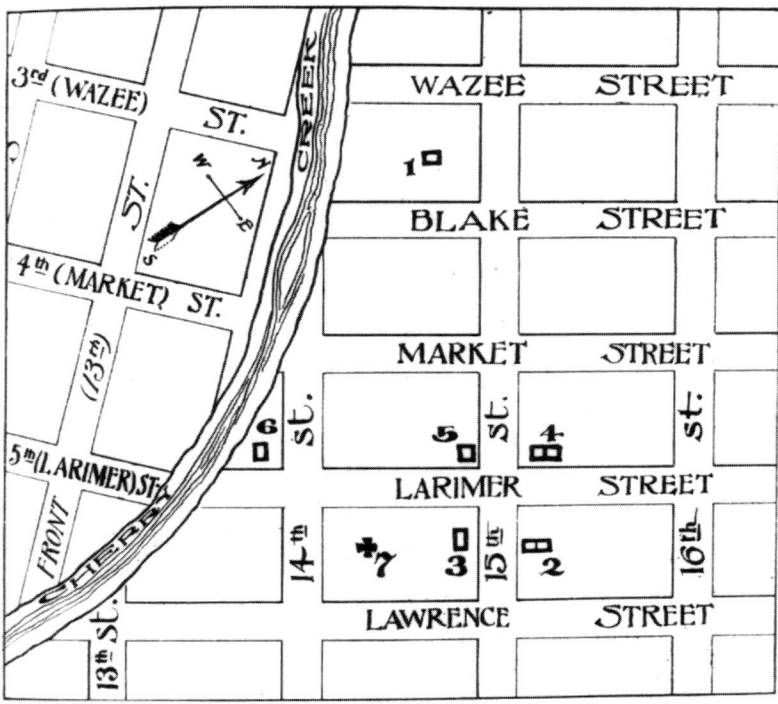

4) *This map shows the location of the earliest pioneer structures in Denver City including the unfinished cabin of Charles Nichols at point number 1 that marked the short-lived St. Charles Town Company. Point number 2 is the Moyne and Rice cabin. Mark number 3 shows the location of General William Larimer's cabin. Point 4 shows the Lawrence and Dorsett cabins, and point 5 is the Hickory Rogers cabin. E. P. Stout built his cabin along Cherry Creek at point number 6. Point number 7 marks the spot where the first survey stake was driven by the St. Charles men. (The Denver Public Library, Western History Department)*

Larimer jumped the claim of the previous founders of the short-lived town of St. Charles. When the lone guard, Charles Nichols, protested, the Larimer group gave him the choice of joining them or bending a limb of the nearest cottonwood tree at the end of a rope. Nichols acquiesced.

In less than a week, on November 22, 1858, Larimer formed the Denver City Town Company, named after James Denver, governor of Kansas Territory of which the area was a part. Actually, Denver had resigned a few weeks earlier, but the pioneers had no way of knowing that. Coincidentally, James Denver had just sent another official group to the western reaches of his domain. Three men in the group were to act as county officers of the newly formed Arapahoe County and had arrived at Auraria the same day as the Larimer party.

E. P. Stout was President of the town company and William Larimer was Secretary and Donating Agent, which authorized him to give two lots to anyone who would build a 16-foot-by-16-foot cabin. Larimer and his son built their cabins on Larimer Street with logs cut from the cottonwoods near Cherry Creek. Later, General Larimer and D. C. Collier crossed the Platte River to the northwest and staked out the town of Highland.

5) *This is a view of Denver around 1867 looking north from the corner of 14th and Arapahoe streets. The back corner of the Methodist-Episcopal Church is visible on the left. (Courtesy of First Interstate Bank)*

By 1859 the towns were formed, land divided, and the real estate speculators, promoters, and merchants waited for the gold rush to happen. Until that time, only a modest amount of gold had been found in the South Platte River and other streams. Interest in the area was originally sparked in the east by small samples of gold-bearing soil taken from the Russell camp to Kansas City where it was proof of Rocky Mountain gold. Rumors of vast riches in the region were confirmed when John Gregory, in May 1859, found veins of gold in a mountain gulch that was to become Black Hawk and Central City. When news of this discovery reached the east, the "rush to the Rockies" was on.

Building a Prairie Town

After spending the last 45 days on the trail, Mrs. Henry C. Brown told her husband that she was going no farther. They were on their way to California from St. Joseph, Missouri, when they stopped the oxen-driven wagon on a hill east of the new settlement of Denver City in June 1860. They saw a few cabins on the banks of the river and the Rocky Mountains beyond, stretching as far north and south as they could see. Mrs. Brown was tired. Evidently so was her husband because they decided to end their journey. Between them and the settlement was a steep hill. Although he didn't know it at the time, at the base of the hill Henry Brown would build the elegant hotel which today bears his name. Up the rise and a little to the south, the state capitol would stand on land homesteaded and donated by Brown.

Henry Cordes Brown was a builder. He had learned carpentry at an early age in St. Louis and had dabbled in architecture there. He had worked with his brother, who was an architect and builder, until he decided to strike out on his own in 1852. For eight years he had traveled from St. Louis to California, to Oregon, to South America, to the northeast, and finally to St. Joseph. During his travels he had been involved in several business ventures including a sawmill in Washington state, a practice as an architect and builder in San Francisco, and an unsuccessful attempt to organize the Decatur Town Company in Nebraska.

Brown's first project in Denver was the construction of a large building on the banks of Cherry Creek that he leased to the Methodist Episcopal congregation, only a small contingent of the barely 1,000 pioneers who inhabited Denver City at the time.

Henry Brown was typical of the many pioneers working hard in the latter part of the century to make Denver a livable town after the initial gold

6) Henry C. Brown arrived in Denver on June 9, 1860, with his wife and daughter. At that time the only substantial building was the Broadwell Hotel at 16th and Larimer. Brown began to ply his trade as a builder and developer, culminating in the construction of the Brown Palace Hotel. He also donated a portion of his homesteaded land for the site of the State Capitol. (The Denver Public Library, Western History Department)

fever had worn off. The miners seeking their fortunes were now in the mountains, no longer panning for gold in Cherry Creek or the Platte River. Denver City residents were supplying the miners with goods and services and taking care of the people in the struggling new town that had consolidated with Auraria in April 1860 to become the one town of Denver. Although mining, population growth, and the general economic conditions slowed in the 1860s, Denverites spent the decade extending the city, building places to work and live, providing for water and other services, and establishing the basis for an economy that would thrive in the 1870s.

Shortly after forming the Denver City Town Company, Colonel Samuel Curtis, one of Larimer's party and a founding member of Denver City, laid out the city's first streets, tapping his experience as a civil engineer. Using a rope for a surveyor's chain, Curtis established a base line using a path that was a trail for wagon trains coming from towns along the Missouri River to Denver City. This became 15th Street, which at that time was called F Street. At a right angle to this street, he established another street in front of Larimer's cabin, which has since been known by the General's name. He surveyed other streets in the area parallel to 15th and Larimer streets. All of the downtown streets which are numbered today were originally labeled with letters, starting with A Street (10th Street) at Cherry Creek and running northeast to S Street.

By 1860, Denver had been platted as far east as 28th Street south to about 12th Avenue, although at that time Colfax and Broadway did not exist so the rectangular grid did not change to the north-south orientation it has today.

In Auraria, the streets were based on the numbered streets parallel to Cherry Creek. Named cross streets were perpendicular to those. This was slightly off the Denver City grid, which suited the Auraria founders because of their early rivalry with Denver City. Highland, northwest across the Platte, was also laid out by William Larimer in December 1858 shortly after Denver City, although the layout of the streets did not correspond to what they are today. Highland became a part of Denver when Auraria did.

The pioneers who arrived in the new settlement called Denver built their cabins and crude commercial buildings with logs cut from willow

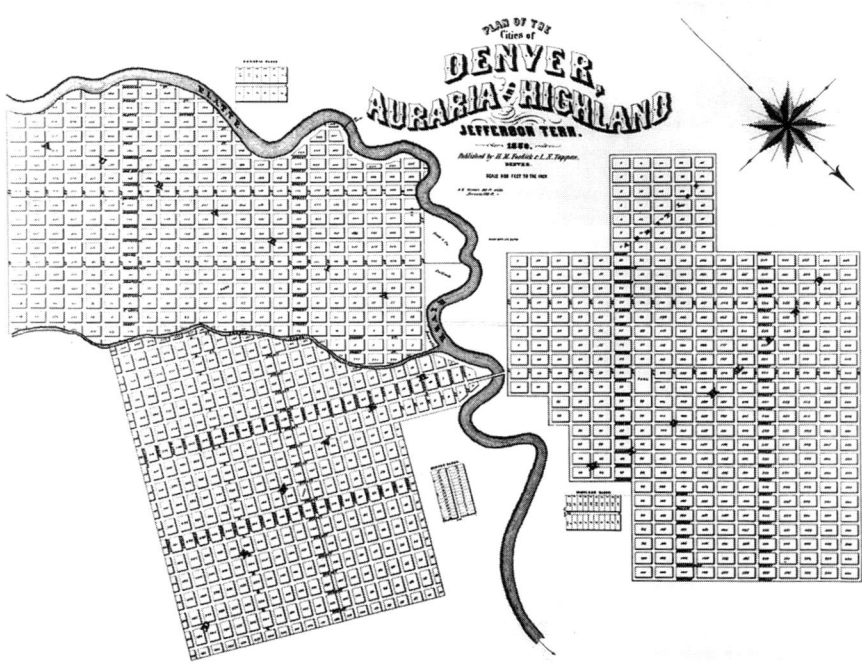

7) By 1860, three towns had been platted around the confluence of the South Platte River and Cherry Creek: Denver City, Auraria, and Highland. The three towns consolidated into one town, Denver, in April 1860. In 1875, the town of Highlands (with an "s") was formed, but was annexed to Denver on June 22, 1896. (Courtesy, Colorado Historical Society)

and cottonwood trees that grew near the rivers. However, trees were scarce and the rough cabins provided little protection from the harsh winters. Instead, the pioneers turned to brick as a building material. Because there was an abundance of clay in the area, bricks were plentiful and often less expensive than lumber. Some brick houses were constructed as early as 1860, but many of the buildings in the early part of the decade were still built from wood.

A fire on April 19, 1863, changed all that. It began near 15th and Blake and burned much of the business district, causing more than $250,000 in damage. After that, construction of frame buildings in the business district was prohibited by law. A larger fire in 1864 once again caused people to rethink the wisdom of building with wood anywhere in the city. Availability and the threat of fire, along with extra protection from feared Indian raids, started the tradition of Denver as a brick city.

Another disaster in 1864 changed life along Cherry Creek. That river had always appeared to be a sandy wash with just a trickle of water. However, after a few days of heavy rain, Cherry Creek and the South Platte flooded on May 20, 1864. The low-lying areas of Auraria were inundated and structures in the creek bed washed away. Henry Brown's Methodist church, the City Hall, and the Rocky Mountain News building were among the casualties.

8) Many early settlers unwisely built their homes and businesses in the Cherry Creek river bed. They learned how quickly weather and natural conditions can change in Colorado on May 20, 1864, when a flood washed away nearly every structure in its path. (The Denver Public Library, Western History Department)

During the 1860s Denver's business district grew slowly, reflecting the flagging mining industry. Most of the structures were two- and three-story buildings built of brick with simple facades. The Clark, Gruber & Company private mint (1860), National Block (1865), Brendlinger Block (1867), and the Fillmore Block (1868) were typical of the utilitarian work of the early builders like Henry Brown. A notable exception was the Lawrence Street Methodist Church, built at 14th and Arapahoe in 1864. As the town's first real church building, it was built in the Gothic style with engaged buttresses and brick spires and appeared more decorative than most of the crude buildings of the day.

9) *Because wood was scarce and subject to fires, most of the buildings in early Denver were constructed of brick. The designs were simple but sturdy, and many are still standing today. This late 1860s view is looking down Market Street. A stagecoach is parked on 15th Street in front of the Wells Fargo Express office on the corner. The three-story Tappan building on the left served as the state capitol for a short time. (Courtesy of First Interstate Bank)*

10) *After the arrival of the railroad in 1870, local builders had a wider range of materials to choose from. Many of the buildings in Larimer Square date from this period and have been renovated. While still using brick as their major building material, these buildings are more ornate than their predecessors.*

When the railroad arrived in 1870, Denver changed greatly. After the arrival of the railroad a wider range of building materials was available, most notably iron, and a broader range of ideas about architectural style and design came with the newly arriving settlers. The railroad also brought more people, more industry, and established Denver as a transportation center of the west.

As railroads were extended into the mountains to service the mines in surrounding states as well as Colorado, ore could be brought to the city for smelting. In 1878, Nathaniel Hill built the Argo smelter north of the downtown area. Shortly thereafter, the Argo was joined by the Omaha and Grant Smelter and the Globe Smelting and Refining company built by Dennis Sheedy. By 1890, the smelters were Denver's largest industry, their prominent brick smokestacks belching a dark and sulfurous smoke.

Another surge in growth came in the 1880s caused by increased silver production in Leadville in the late 1870s and the broadening of Denver's economic base. More people came to Denver lured by its healthy climate, opportunity, and promise of riches. One miner in particular changed the look of the city. Horace A. W. Tabor had come to Colorado in 1859 and had taken up mining in Leadville. After making his fortune in silver mining, he had been elected lieutenant governor in 1878 and moved to Denver. He built the Tabor Block at 16th and Larimer in 1880, which was the first building over four stories high. The Tabor Block sported an elevator and the city's first telephone switchboard. Tabor also built the Tabor Grand Opera House, considered one of the finest theaters in America at the time.

11) The Tabor Block, at 16th and Larimer, was built in 1880 by Horace Tabor after he made his fortune in silver mining. Frank E. Edbrooke, one of Denver's most famous early architects, supervised construction and may have had a hand in its design. Designed in the Second Empire style, the Tabor Block was one of the city's first "tall" buildings. It was demolished in 1972.(Courtesy of First Interstate Bank)

Other prominent commercial buildings completed during the 1880s and early 1890s included the Union Station at the end of 17th Street (1881), the Arapahoe County Courthouse at 16th and Tremont (1883), The Denver Club Building at 17th and Welton (1889), the Boston Building (1889), the Mining Exchange Building (1891), and the Equitable Building (1892).

12) Still in use today, the Equitable Building was built for the Equitable Life Insurance Company in 1892. Its floor plan is in the shape of back to back "E"s. It is one of the best examples of the Italian Renaissance Revival style in Denver and has a beautiful lobby with Tiffany glass, Byzantine mosaics, and brass fixtures.

13) The Boston Building as it appears today lacks its original cornice, a third-floor balcony above the 17th Street entrance, and some of its early ornamentation. It was built in 1889 as the Boston Block.

14) The Kittredge Building at 16th and Glenarm Place was constructed in 1890 by C. H. Kittredge as an office building with retail space on the first floor. When the Paramount theater was built in 1930 along Glenarm Place, a portion of the Kittredge Building near the alley was used as the main entrance to the theater. The entrance was closed when the building was remodeled, making the Glenarm Place entrance the entry used today.

Denver's residential neighborhoods grew as rapidly as the commercial blocks. In the early 1860s, most of the frame and brick houses were built near Cherry Creek, oftentimes shoulder-to-shoulder with the commercial buildings. Even the homes of the wealthy and famous were near the business blocks. The first house of John Evans, second territorial governor of Colorado, was on 14th Street as was that of water company organizer and railroad builder David Moffat.

As the business area grew, many people built south and southeast of the developing business center due to the unsuitability of northern land near the Platte River for homes. Streets were extended to the foot of Capitol Hill near what is now Colfax and Broadway, but stopped there because it was impractical to continue the street grid up the hill. A farmer named Thomas Skerritt established the beginnings of Broadway in 1870. Skerritt had a farm in present-day Englewood and he needed access to water, so he plowed a road from his home north to Cherry Creek. The road was later extended farther north to Denver and became the baseline for laying out the north-south/east-west street grid up Capitol Hill and east to where Aurora is today.

15) *The Byers-Evans house at 13th and Bannock streets was built in 1883 by William N. Byers, founder of the* Rocky Mountain News. *Byers sold the house in 1889 to William Evans, son of John Evans, who was the second Territorial Governor of Colorado. The house remained in the Evans family until 1981, when it was donated to the Colorado Historical Society. It now houses the society's Denver History Museum.*

Several developers saw the chance to make money carving up the area around early Denver City to make room for the new residents. One of the early ones was Henry Brown. Two years after arriving in Denver, he seized an opportunity courtesy of the federal government. The Homestead Act of 1862 made it possible for him to preempt up to 160 acres if he would live on it for six months. He selected a narrow strip of land on a hill overlooking Denver, the same hill he and his wife had descended when they decided to make Denver their home.

The site stretched from what is now 11th Street to 20th Street and from present-day Broadway to Grant Street. He paid the going government price of $2.50 per acre and filed his claim on April 15, 1864. Brown was doubly fortunate that year because just two weeks before the great flood of Cherry Creek, he moved from his previous home near the creek bed to a house he had built at 12th and Sherman streets. His homestead became known as Brown's bluff.

Brown waited for several years and tried to develop his land, but was unsuccessful. The population of Denver did not increase in the 1860s and actually decreased by more than 1,000 people by 1866.

16) Henry Brown's homestead was about one mile high. This fact is marked on the upper steps of the west side of the Capitol building with a brass marker exactly one mile above sea level. The step with the words incised in it was placed in 1947, but in 1969 students from the engineering school of Colorado State University found the original marker to be about two feet low.

Brown soon recognized another opportunity. Colorado had achieved territorial status in 1861 and had a legislature to govern its affairs. Golden had been the temporary location of the legislature since 1862, but an act of the Seventh Legislative assembly on December 9, 1867, made Denver the official capital. Part of the same act authorized the governor to appoint a three-man commission to select a site for a capitol building. Because the new territory was short of cash, the catch was that the land had to be a gift to Colorado of at least ten acres.

When Henry Brown heard this he quickly realized how he could turn his sand hill into a profitable venture. He offered to donate ten acres of his land to the territory with the stipulation that it only be used as a site for the Capitol. Brown openly stated that his purpose was to increase the property values of his remaining land and establish leverage by which he could force the City of Denver to accept his desired north-south, east-west platting of streets and blocks, unlike the angle platting of existing streets in the business area. Such a layout would not only make the streets easier to build up the hill, it would also provide a greater number of choice building sites for Brown to sell.

Brown deeded his property to the territory on January 11, 1868. The next 19 years involved waiting and legal disputes between Brown and the state. Colorado was finally given complete title to the land on January 4, 1886.

While the legal proceedings were under way, Denver had become the official choice for the state capitol in an election in 1881. Between that time and 1886, a Board of Direction and Supervision for the new building was formed, land titles were verified, money was raised, and an architect was selected. Detroit architect Elijah E. Myers was chosen based on an architectural competition held in 1885. Finally, in July of 1886 excavation for the Capitol on Brown's Bluff was started. On July 4, 1890, the cornerstone was laid during a great, daylong celebration.

Most of the construction work on the Capitol was completed by June 1898, although the legislature was supposed to move into its space in January 1895. The Capitol was designed in the federal revival style and

17) *This 1889 view of the State Capitol shows the brick structure for the rotunda rising within the exterior walls. More than 5,000,000 bricks were used along with 230,000 cubic feet of granite for the walls and 332,600 cubic feet of stone for the foundation. There are 210 tons of cast iron columns and 315 tons of steel beams. (The Denver Public Library, Western History Department)*

planned in the shape of a Greek cross, 383 feet in the long dimension and 313 feet in the short dimension.

One of the most distinctive features was, and still is, the gold dome. The gold was actually an afterthought and originated as both a symbolic gesture and a practical matter. The architect who was hired as supervising architect after Myers was dismissed, Frank Edbrooke, suggested Colorado gold, symbolizing the commodity that had founded the state. Pragmatically, he had decided after various tests of bronze paints and lacquers on copper sheets that these were not suitable for roofing material and decided on gold instead. The original gold coating totaled 200 ounces (12½ pounds) and was applied in 1908. Since then, new gold leaf has been applied several times to maintain its brilliant luster.

18) This office was typical of the original interior of the State Capitol when most of the construction was completed in 1898. Frank Edbrooke took over the job of supervising architect after the original architect, E. E. Myers, was dismissed. (The Denver Public Library, Western History Department)

19) The State Capitol has been beautifully maintained and restored in recent years. The wainscoting of the first three floors is Colorado onyx, a rare stone found in huge boulders in a small area near Beulah, Colorado. The entire supply of this beautiful variegated pink stone was used for the Capitol, and no more is known to exist.

Henry Brown's early homesteading, platting, and land donation to the territory did encourage expansion of the residential area up Capitol Hill. Later, some of the wealthiest and most influential people in Denver history would make Capitol Hill their home, dotting it with mansions that remain today.

Denver's population stagnated in the 1860s, reaching 4,759 in 1870, only ten more people than in 1860. With the arrival of the railroad in 1870, however, Denver's population exploded, climbing to more than 35,000 in 1880 and more than 106,000 by 1890. Residential areas sprang up in several directions.

The original area that William Larimer had platted as Highland languished until the late 1860s, but grew rapidly after 1870. Small homes and mansions alike dotted the hills overlooking the Platte River and central Denver. Schools, churches, and businesses followed. In 1875, the Highland Park Company was formed by Dr. William A. Bell, General William J. Palmer, and other railroad builders from Colorado Springs. They planned a roughly diagonal area from Speer Boulevard (then called Lake Avenue) north to 38th Avenue and from what is now Zuni Street west to Lowell Boulevard. The final development only extended to Federal Boulevard. The streets were given Scottish names and planned as a series of curves, some of which remain today. On the west side of Federal Boulevard, all that remains of the development is Highland Park surrounded by a few curved streets of the original plan.

As Highland Park developed, the local residents decided to incorporate as a town separate from Denver. In 1875, the town of Highlands (with an s) was formed and extended from Zuni Street (then called Gallup Avenue) west to Lowell Boulevard. In 1890, the western boundary was extended to Sheridan Boulevard, the division between Arapahoe and Jefferson Counties. The southern boundary was Colfax Avenue and the northern boundary was 38th Avenue (then Prospect Avenue). Ultimately, Highlands' residents voted to be annexed to Denver on June 22, 1896.

20) Highland Park Place just west of Federal Boulevard is one of the few curved streets remaining from the original layout of Highland Park. It later became part of the town of Highlands, which was annexed to Denver in 1896.

21) As streetcar lines were extended out from the center of Denver in the 1870s and 1880s, more distant neighborhoods began to spring up. Some of the earliest were northeast of the downtown area like Curtis Park and the Clements neighborhood, shown in this photograph. Many of the early houses have been restored. A few are highly rated bed and breakfast establishments.

Other towns and subdivisions that enterprising developers formed in the 1870s and 1880s included Curtis Park, North Capitol Hill, City Park, Montclair, and Park Hill to the east. Argo, Swansea, and Globeville developed north, as housing for the many immigrants working the smelters, while South Denver incorporated a large area south of Alameda to Yale, from Pecos to Colorado Boulevard. The towns and developments that were not annexed to Denver separately were later consolidated when the City and County of Denver was formed in 1902.

While gold had created Denver and lured many to the area with promises of riches, the pioneers soon discovered something more precious than the yellow metal: water. On the high plains where the average annual precipitation is barely 14 inches, people needed water to drink and to irrigate gardens, yards, and farms. In the early 1860s, Denver residents got their drinking water out of the Platte River or Cherry Creek (when it wasn't dry) or dug their own wells. It wasn't long, however, before pollution in the rivers became a problem and the water table started to drop because of all the wells being dug. Some shops and private companies got their water from springs or sources away from town and sold it in bottles or hauled it into town in water wagons.

By the end of the decade it was obvious that a better system was needed, and many people tried to get rich by supplying Denver with piped water. The first was Col. James Archer. Archer was a prominent businessman who helped bring the Kansas Pacific Railroad to Denver in addition to founding a gas works that supplied early Denver houses and streets with gas illumination.

Walter Cheesman, David Moffat, and Archer formed the Denver City Water Company on October 30, 1870, and began pumping water in January 1872. They built a pump house about where 15th Street intersected the Platte River and got their water through shallow wells supplied by the Platte. They used a steam-powered pump to supply the water through four miles of pipes. Unfortunately, the water wasn't very pure. Many people fitted their faucets with strainers to catch small fish, and in 1879 the impure water contributed to a typhoid outbreak.

Archer expanded the company in 1878 and tried to supply cleaner water by getting it farther upstream on the Platte. He built a ditch to carry water to Lake Archer, a half-mile long holding reservoir he built east of the Platte between Ellsworth and Eighth Avenues. From there, water was pumped throughout Denver City Water Company's mains. The buildings that housed the pumps are still used by the Denver Water Department at 12th and Shoshone.

22) The Denver City Water Company got its water from a well next to the Platte River. The 15th Street pump station (also called the Holly Water Works) was constructed in 1871 and housed the pumps. It was located at 15th and Bassett streets. (Courtesy of Denver Water Department)

In 1883, another source of water was discovered. Richard McCormick was searching for coal when he struck an artesian well just south of the present site of Mile-High Stadium, near 17th and Federal. Elsewhere in North Denver, four artesian wells supplied the Beaver Brook Water Company with clean water for its customers. By 1886, there were more than 130 artesian wells in the Denver area. Even Henry Brown's Brown Palace still has two artesian wells 750 feet deep.

23) Lake Archer was built as a reservoir and settling basin for South Platte River water transported in a ditch from far upstream. The first stone building in the West Side Pump Station complex was built in 1880. Another building was added a year later to house two more pumps. The third building was constructed 24 years later as a boiler house. The West Side Pump Station supplied Denver water through the summer of 1929. These buildings have been used continuously by the Denver Water Department since that time. They were restored in 1983. (Courtesy of Denver Water Department)

For more than two decades, 11 different water companies competed, often bitterly, over who would supply water to the city. Some were successful, some went bankrupt. After James Archer's death, David Moffat and Walter Cheesman left the company and formed the Citizens Water Company in 1889. They got their water from the South Platte Canyon to avoid pollution and built Marston Lake Reservoir southwest of the city. Citizens Water Company managed to survive the competition until 1894, when the remaining water companies consolidated into the Denver Union Water Company with Walter Cheesman as President and David Moffat as Treasurer. The company was sold to the City of Denver in 1918 and is now run by the Board of Water Commissioners.

Both Cheesman and Moffat realized that Denver needed more water than could be supplied by wells and the Platte River. They started to plan for a dam on the South Fork of the South Platte River about 45 miles from Denver to hold melting snowpack. The result was Cheesman Reservoir, completed in 1905. It was the first in a long history of dams and water diversion projects built since then to bring the precious commodity to the eastern plains for an ever-growing metropolitan area.

Adequate drinking water wasn't the only thing that concerned Denver residents. After living in the dry, dusty, nearly treeless settlement for several years, people wanted some greenery and gardens to make life more pleasant. As early as 1859 an article in the *Rocky Mountain News* announced the formation of a ditch company to bring water to the "dry diggings just west of town." Nothing became of this effort, but a year later a group of men incorporated the Capital Hydraulic Company and secured water rights to a portion of the South Platte River. They started construction, but engineering miscalculations forced the promoters to abandon the project.

Several years later, in 1865, Denver businessman John Smith revived the project and called it City Ditch. He tapped into the South Platte near where it exits the mountains and dug a sinuous ditch from there through south Denver, along Capitol Hill and on to where City Park is now. Smith completed the project in 1867. Lateral ditches ran from the ditch to irrigate the young city. Many of the smaller ditches ran down Capitol Hill and into the business and residential areas. The side ditches were between the sidewalks and the streets, spanned by planks at the intersections. For many years Smith leased some of the water to the city, but finally sold it to Denver in 1882.

Where the ditch passed by a shallow depression in South Denver, Smith formed a lake, formally known by his name today, but more generally known as the north lake in Washington Park. The last open portion of City Ditch is visible as it meanders through the park on its way to City Park lake, where it terminates. Elsewhere, it has been enclosed in a buried conduit.

24) In 1867 John Smith brought South Platte River water from southwest of the city to the parched downtown area with the City Ditch. It is shown here in 1936 near where it crosses Downing Street south of South High School. The high water line is near the base of the tree. Where it is still visible in Washington Park, it is popularly known as Smith's Ditch. (Courtesy of Denver Water Department)

Other Denver developers and entrepreneurs built additional irrigation ditches. In the early 1870s Hiram Wolff dug the Highland Ditch, bringing water from the Table Mountain Ditch to northwest Denver. Wolff was an early Highland settler who had a farm and tree nursery near 29th and Lowell. Reservoirs of the ditch system included Berkeley Lake, Rocky Mountain Lake, Sloan's Lake, and Lake Rhoda (in what is today the Lakeside Amusement Park). In 1882, the Highland Ditch became part of the Rocky Mountain Ditch system.

In east and south Denver, investors decided to build the High Line Canal for farm irrigation near property they owned. Built in 1882, it taps the South Platte River, near Waterton southwest of Littleton, and runs for about 71 miles until it ends east of the present-day Rocky Mountain Arsenal. Baron Walter von Richthofen tapped into the High Line Canal at Windsor Lake (now a part of Fairmount Cemetery) to build a ditch to water his parched development of Montclair. Unfortunately, the High Line Canal has junior water rights, so it is usually full only during times of flooding or in especially wet years. Today, much of the High Line Canal is maintained with an adjacent path for walking, jogging, and horseback riding.

25) The High Line Canal is shown here at Big Dry Creek in 1935. The canal was built by British land developers to create farms by selling water with the land. Today, 75 headgates still serve more than 100 customers along the canal. (Courtesy of Denver Water Department)

With water, Denver also needed communication with the "States," as the rest of the country was often called. At first, there was no direct telegraph service. Telegrams were sent by wire to Fort Kearney and forwarded to the city 200 miles by stagecoach. Denver got its first direct telegraph service in October 1863 when messages were sent to an office at 15th and Market streets. There were several telegraph companies for a while, but they eventually merged into the Western Union Company.

The real magic was the telephone. Just a few years after its invention, Denver had its first telephone service. This began on February 26, 1879, and by October of that year the first switchboard opened. By 1881, the city had two telephone companies and 200 subscribers. The switchboards were located in the Tabor Building from 1881 until 1890. As with other utilities, several companies competed, but eventually the Colorado Telephone Company had the monopoly. It later became the Mountain States Telephone and Telegraph Company.

Another electronic marvel was electricity. Denver saw its first incandescent lights demonstrated on April 21, 1880, and by the spring of 1881 the first electric generator was installed at 21st and Wewatta. By 1885, city streets were illuminated by electricity, making Denver the third city in the world to adopt the new invention for street lighting. By 1890, city homes had more than 50,000 electric lights, and the many amusement parks that opened in the 1880s used the lights to their advantage as they do today.

Before electricity, gas was used to light Denver's streets, homes, and businesses. James Archer, who was just getting his water company started, saw even more profits to be made with another utility. In 1871, he formed the Denver Gas Company. At that time the gas was not natural gas, but was manufactured in coal-burning retort houses. Archer's first retort house was located at 18th and Wewatta, from which he supplied gas to the streetlights until they were replaced by electricity.

His franchise expired in 1885, and Archer's company was merged into the Denver Gas and Electric Company, which became Public Service Company of Colorado in 1923. Natural gas didn't replace coal gas until 1928. Until then, the city was dotted with huge gas tanks that stored gas for peak periods of demand. They were more than 100 feet tall and more than 110 feet in diameter, and they expanded up and down as they were filled or emptied.

While the pioneers needed places to live and work and basic city services, they also needed a banking system to take care of the monetary transactions multiplying as fast as the population. While Henry Brown and his wife were crossing the eastern plains nearing Denver, two enterprising banking brothers from Leavenworth, Kansas, had already arrived. Unlike the Browns, the two brothers had a definite reason for moving to Denver. Since 1858, they had been operating a successful business in Kansas. During that time they received increasing quantities of gold dust

26) Before natural gas was available, gas was manufactured by burning coal in retort houses like the one shown here. The gas was stored in huge expanding tanks placed around the city for periods of peak demand. Denver got natural gas service in 1928. (Courtesy of Public Service Company of Colorado)

27) Austin M. Clark was one of the founders of Clark, Gruber & Company, a private mint at 16th and Market streets. The business opened in 1860 and minted gold pieces before there was a law prohibiting private minting of money. (The Denver Public Library, Western History Department)

from the Pikes Peak region. They soon realized that they could make a tidy profit if they established a bank in Denver along with a mint to convert the gold dust and ore into coins.

While their partner, E. H. Gruber, was in Boston buying the necessary dies and presses for the mint, Austin M. and Milton E. Clark came to Denver, arriving in early spring of 1860. They purchased property at the northwest corner of 16th and Market streets and had Henry Brown build a small, two-story brick building to serve the banking needs of the steadily increasing influx of miners and pioneers. On June 20, 1860, the firm of Clark, Gruber and Company opened for business and began minting hefty $10 and $20 gold pieces in the basement.

28) The Clark, Gruber & Company mint was purchased by the United States for its first mint in Denver although no coins were ever stamped by the government here. The banking portion of the original business continued as Clark & Company, which was later purchased by the First National Bank of Denver. This gave rise to the claim that the First National Bank (now First Interstate Bank) is the oldest bank in Colorado. (Courtesy of First Interstate Bank)

Because at the time there was no law that prevented the private minting of money, the three men were doing nothing illegal, and in the best tradition of American enterprise and the West, were meeting a market demand and were making a profit doing it. In the first two years of operation, the new company minted about $3,000,000 worth of gold coins.

The Clark brothers' private mint did not last. In 1864, Congress passed a law prohibiting private coinage of money. Two years earlier, however, it had passed another law creating a United States Mint in Denver. Instead of building their own facility, the federal government bought the minting facilities of Clark, Gruber and Company. Oddly enough, no government coinage was ever done at that mint. Its activities were confined to melting, refining, assaying, and stamping gold bars, which were returned to depositors. In 1869, the mint served only as an assay office.

When private minting was outlawed, Gruber left the firm, and the banking portion of the business continued as Clark & Company. When mining tycoon Jerome Chaffee formed the First National Bank of Denver in May 1865, he acquired the banking business of Clark & Company. David Moffat became a cashier at the bank in 1866 and ultimately became its president. The name was changed in 1971 to First of Denver and again in 1982 to IntraWest Bank of Denver. Today it operates as First Interstate Bank.

29) The original First National Bank building was constructed in 1865 at 15th and Blake streets. A third floor was added in the early 1870s. The Colorado Constitutional Convention was held in the building from December 1875 until March 1876. The building continued in use until April 1977, when it was burned by an arsonist's fire and had to be demolished. (Courtesy of First Interstate Bank)

Elsewhere, several other banks were founded to meet the growing financial needs of the miners and the exploding city population. Charles Kountze and his brother, Luther, formed the Kountze Brothers Bank in 1862 and occupied a building at 15th and Blake. They received a charter in 1866 and became the Colorado National Bank. After a 23-year stay at 17th and Larimer, Colorado National Bank moved to its present site at 17th and Champa. Colorado National remained one of the state's last major independent banking companies until 1993, when Colorado National Bankshares was purchased by Minneapolis-based First Bank System.

Even Henry Brown got into the banking business for a short time when he formed the Bank of Denver with C. D. Gurley. Brown opened his bank on January 1, 1873, in a corner of his *Tribune* building where he was also in the newspaper business. He was president of the bank, but sold his interest at the end of the year. For 25 years banks did a prosperous business, and Denver thrived until the crash of 1893.

Transportation at the Crossroads of the West

The settlers, developers, and bankers of early Denver knew the importance of the city's geographic position. They knew that in order to survive, they needed contact with the rest of the country. In addition to communication, they needed supplies and a way to sell and transport the riches of their mines. Although Denver was at first isolated, they also knew its location held a strategic position in the expanding west.

As early as November 19, 1858, less than a month after Denver City was formed, William Larimer wrote to H. B. Denman, the Mayor of the City of Leavenworth: "This is the point also where the Santa Fe and New Mexico road crosses to Fort Laramie and Fort Bridger, also the great leading road from the Missouri River: In short, it is the center of all the great leading thoroughfares and is bound to be the great city. The mountains are within 12 or 15 miles of it and form the most beautiful view ever looked upon." One hundred and thirty years later another prominent citizen, Mayor Federico Peña, imagined a great city and pushed for construction of Denver International Airport, midway between Europe and the Pacific Rim and between Canada and Mexico, its tent-roofed terminal within sight of the majestic Rocky Mountains.

Denver as a transportation hub started simply enough. General Larimer and his partners knew Denver had to be connected with the country's transportation network. To encourage service, they gave 53 lots and nine shares of the town company to the Leavenworth and Pikes Peak

30) Denver's first connection to the outside world was with wagon trains and stagecoaches. A popular gathering spot for wagon trains in the early 1860s was the Elephant Corral on Blake Street between 14th and 15th. It was adjacent to the Denver House hotel. (Courtesy, Colorado Historical Society)

Express stagecoach line. The Express started service on May 7, 1859, carrying passengers, mail, and freight. For larger shipments of freight and transportation of settlers, oxen wagon trains regularly made the trip across the prairie.

In less than a year the Leavenworth and Pikes Peak Express went bankrupt, but service was assumed by the Central Overland California and Pike's Peak Express. It used the Planter's House at 16th and Blake streets as a depot and post office. By this time, Blake Street was emerging as the center of business, commerce and transportation in the young town.

The Central Overland line suffered the same fate as its predecessor and was sold at auction to Ben Holladay, who formed the Holladay Overland Mail & Express Company in 1863. He built a new depot at 15th and McGaa, which was later renamed to Holladay Street in his honor. It remained that way for 20 years until it was renamed Market Street.

Although the stagecoach and wagon trains supplied Denver with basic necessities, their capacity was limited, travel time slow, and they were vulnerable to Indian raids. Business leaders and developers knew Denver needed connection with the coming transcontinental railroad. However, early surveys along Colorado's Continental Divide were not encouraging. High peaks and winter snow convinced the Union Pacific to choose a northern route, through Cheyenne, for their coast-to-coast railroad, where the route through the Wyoming mountains was much easier.

31) Before the railroad, passengers arrived in Denver by stagecoach. The Central Overland California and Pike's Peak Express used the Planter's House at 16th and Blake streets beginning in 1860. After the company went bankrupt a few years later, the building survived as a hotel until it was destroyed by a fire in 1875. (Courtesy, Colorado Historical Society; Photo by William Chamberlain)

Denver citizens knew that the decision could mark the end for their new town unless they did something. In response to this fear and to protect their investments, John Evans, Walter Cheesman, David Moffat, William Byers, and others formed the Denver Pacific Railway to connect Denver with the transcontinental line in Cheyenne. Even Henry Brown had a hand in its organization. Construction started in May 1868, and the first iron horse rolled into Denver on June 22, 1870.

After the first railroad linked Denver, others quickly followed. In August 1870, the Kansas Pacific Railroad started operation, connecting Denver with Kansas City and St. Louis. The Colorado Central Railroad built narrow-gauge tracks from Golden to Boulder and Fort Collins and extended into the mountain mining towns of Black Hawk, Central City, and Georgetown. William Jackson Palmer organized the Denver & Rio Grande Railway to establish a north-south route along the front range and into New Mexico. He founded Colorado Springs to help finance construction. Some of his lines extended west into the mining areas in the southwestern part of the state, including the towns of Durango and Silverton.

John Evans also established the Denver & New Orleans Railroad and, with David Moffat and Walter Cheesman, built the South Park & Pacific Railway. The South Park line served Park and Summit counties, including the ore-rich town of Leadville.

32) *The first railroad station at the foot of 17th Street was built in 1881. Across the street were the Denver City Railway Company carbarn and stables. (Courtesy, Colorado Historical Society)*

The effects of the railroad coming to Colorado were immediate. The population of Denver exploded from 4,759 in 1870 to more than 35,000 by 1880. The state's population jumped from about 40,000 to almost 200,000 in the same decade. The railroad made it easy to bring ore from the mountains to Denver for smelting. It also encouraged the development of the eastern plains for ranching and farming, making Denver a center for food-processing plants, flour mills, and stockyards. The railroad also made it easier for people to visit and move to Denver and to import more goods for the growing town.

When the railroad first came to Denver, several depots served the various lines. The Kansas Pacific Depot, built at 22nd and Wynkoop, served the Denver Pacific and the Colorado Central as well as trains of the Kansas Pacific. George J. Gould, who controlled the Denver, Rio Grande, and other lines, thought one station should serve all the lines. To this end, he organized the Union Depot and Railroad Company to build the first union station. Opened on June 1, 1881, the station was built at the foot of 17th Street where the present terminal is. A fire in March 1894 destroyed the central part, which was rebuilt with a larger tower than the original.

In 1912, the Denver Union Terminal Railway Company was formed out of the reorganization of the previous station company. The central portion was again rebuilt as the station that stands today.

33) Union Station today has changed little from when it was built in 1912, replacing the previous station. In 1906, the famous "Mizpah" arch was constructed at Wynkoop Street. The bronzed steel arch was 65 feet high and 86 feet wide, and was illuminated by 1,600 lights. Above the arch on the Union Station side was the word "Welcome," while on the 17th Street side was the Hebrew word "Mizpah," which roughly translates to "may the Lord keep watch between you and me when we are out of each other's sight." The arch was removed in 1931.

34) David Moffat (seated in chair) poses with his First National Bank employees near the turn of the century. Moffat started as a cashier in the bank. He also helped form the Denver City Water Company and the Denver Pacific Railway. He is best known for building the Denver, Northwestern & Pacific Railroad. The Moffat tunnel is named in his honor. (Courtesy of First Interstate Bank)

One maverick railroad builder was David Moffat. After he had helped form some of the early rail lines, his dream late in life was to build a railroad through the coal-rich northwestern part of the state from Denver to Salt Lake City. There it could join with another railroad being built by William Clark of Montana and extend to the Pacific. Beginning in 1902 until his death in 1911, Moffat built his Denver, Northwestern & Pacific Railroad, better known as the Moffat Road, as far as Steamboat Springs. The most difficult stretch of track was scaling the Continental Divide over Rollins Pass. The pass was difficult to traverse in the best of winter conditions and was often closed by snow from early fall to late spring.

Moffat had a difficult time building his railroad. He was in competition with the Union Pacific as well as the Denver & Rio Grande. His competitors didn't want him to complete his line and made it difficult to get loans from eastern sources. Moffat borrowed heavily from his own First National Bank and ultimately died bankrupt. His successors at the bank barely saved that institution from insolvency.

Moffat's competitors even prevented him from using Union Station. Instead, he built the Moffat Depot at 15th and Bassett streets, which it used until the line merged with the Rio Grande in 1947.

David Moffat's greatest legacy is the tunnel with his name. After his death the railroad was extended to Craig, but the cost of keeping the railroad in service over Rollins Pass in the winter consumed each year's profits. The government finally recognized the importance of transporting coal and oil from that part of the state during World War I. As a result,

35) When David Moffat was prevented from using Union Station by his competitors, he built his own station at 15th and Bassett streets. Although in some disrepair, the building still stands today.

the Moffat Tunnel Improvement District was established by the state legislature to levy taxes, issue bonds, and get the tunnel built. After five years of difficult construction, the Moffat Tunnel was completed in early 1928, avoiding the treacherous journey over the pass above it.

About the same time the railroad connected Denver to the rest of the country, the city was getting its own local transportation system. Before public transportation was available, few people could live far from the center of town unless they had their own horse and carriage. The coming of the streetcar system made it possible for suburbs to spring up around central Denver. Highland, Argo, Swansea, Globeville, Park Hill, Montclair, Harman, Barnum, South Denver, and other neighborhoods can trace their beginnings to the coming of the streetcar.

In December 1871, the Denver Horse Railroad Company started service. Built by Chicago financier Lewis C. Ellsworth, the first line ran from Seventh and Larimer in Auraria up Larimer to its carbarn and stables near Curtis. From there it turned to Champa and continued northeast to 27th Street. Ellsworth Avenue was later named for the builder of the first public transportation system in Denver.

A year later the company was renamed the Denver City Railway, and by 1874 several lines stretched in all directions from the center of town to the new suburbs. To serve the expanding system, the company built a carbarn and stables at 17th and Wynkoop, across the street from Union Station. The building still stands, somewhat altered after a recent renovation for lofts.

When the company would not service 15th Street, the Denver Electric and Cable Company was formed in 1885. Initially, it used a new system developed by Sidney Short, who was a professor at Denver University. The

36) Now called The Streetcar Stables, the building at 17th and Wynkoop streets has recently been remodeled into lofts. It was originally the carbarn and stables for the Denver City Railway Company, which served the city with horse-drawn trolleys. Compare this photograph with photograph 32, Chapter 1.

electric car got its power from a cable laid in a slot between the rails. Unfortunately, when pedestrians or horses stepped on the electrified slot and one of the rails, they got a nasty shock. The system was abandoned within a few years and was replaced with a horse-drawn system. Shortly after its formation, the company was renamed the Denver Tramway Corporation (DTC) in 1886. One of its directors was Henry Brown.

A short time later, New York interests took control of Denver City Railway and renamed it Denver City Cable Railway Company. They began using the new cable car system that had been invented in San Francisco. The company built its huge powerhouse at 18th and Lawrence streets, which still stands, and laid cable lines along Larimer, West Colfax, Kalamath, 17th Avenue, and Welton Street. Along with the cable lines of the rival Denver Tramway Company, Denver had one of the most extensive cable car systems in the country.

Both horse-drawn trolleys and cable cars were eventually replaced by electric trolleys. The first electric streetcar started service in 1889, and within a few years, lines extended to all parts of the city as well as into the outlying cities like Englewood, Golden, and Boulder with the interurban lines. Downtown, on 15th Street between Lawrence and Arapahoe, the Denver Tramway Company in 1892 built the Central Loop, where passengers could transfer between lines. A bustling center of markets, shops, restaurants, and hotels developed around the Loop, making it one of the most active places downtown for many years.

37) The magnificent brick building that stands at 18th and Lawrence was built by the Denver City Cable Railway Company in 1889 for a power house, carbarn, and corporate offices. A portion of Denver's short-lived cable car system was powered from this building.

38) Steel-wheeled electric trolley car number 339 and its motorman pose at the Central Loop in 1949. The Loop was built in 1892 as a place for passengers to transfer between lines. It was on 15th Street between Lawrence and Arapahoe streets. (Photo courtesy Regional Transportation District)

After the depression of 1893, many of the streetcar companies went out of business. By 1900, Denver Tramway Company had taken control of Denver City Cable and other lines, and was the dominant transportation company running electric streetcars exclusively.

39) The powerhouse for the Denver Tramway Company's cable car system was on the southwest corner of Colfax and Broadway. A portion of the building, after it was converted into shops prior to being razed for the Civic Center, can be seen in photograph 2, Chapter 2.

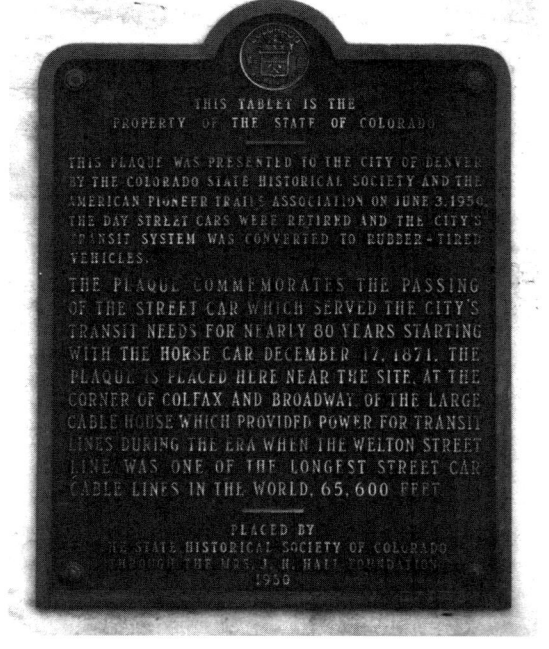

Education and the Arts in Early Denver

As a young town, Denver could not survive only on mining, industry, banking, and the bare necessities of life. Almost as soon as General Larimer founded the city, newly arriving residents began to look for the amenities that made life on the prairie bearable. First among these was a way to educate their children.

Owen J. Goldrick was Denver's first teacher. He raised private money and opened the first school in a cabin in Auraria in August 1859 with 13 students. Less than a year later, Miss Indiana Sopris started another school on May 7, 1860, in a single room on Ferry Street, near 11th Street (about where St. Elizabeth's Church is today on the Auraria campus).

Throughout the 1860s, Denver's children were educated in whatever room or building happened to be available. Most of the schools were privately financed because of limited public funds. Two school districts were established in 1862, with Cherry Creek as the dividing line. The Board of Directors of the East Denver district opened a free school on September 6, 1965, in a building on G Street (16th) between McGaa (Market) and Larimer, and the first school in West Denver opened the same year in the old Federal Arsenal Building at 11th and Lawrence streets.

The Sisters of Loretto and Father Joseph Machebeuf organized the first private school, St. Mary's Academy, in 1864. Higher education began when the Colorado Seminary opened in a two-story brick building on the southwest corner of 14th and Arapahoe streets. Under the leadership of Governor John Evans, the Seminary was organized by the Methodist Episcopal Church. Because of limited funds the school temporary closed in 1867, but it was the beginning of the University of Denver.

Public education did not really expand until the 1870s. What could be considered Denver's first substantial school building opened in 1872 as the Arapahoe School. It was on the north side of Arapahoe, between 17th and 18th streets. For early Denver, it was a handsome three-story brick building with stone trim and a central cupola. A year later, Aaron Gove became superintendent of School District Number 1. He remained head of Denver schools until his retirement in 1904, during which time he oversaw the consolidation of a dozen different school jurisdictions into one school district.

In addition to the Arapahoe School, the Ashland School in Highland opened in 1873, the Broadway School in 1875, and Central School in 1880. Upper-grade classes moved out of the Arapahoe School in January 1882 into the new East Side High School at 19th and Stout streets, and

40) Arapahoe School, constructed in 1872, was Denver's first public school. It included a library, elementary grades, and the first high school in the district. It was closed after just nine years as the business district began to grow around it. (The Denver Public Library, Western History Department)

the Franklin School opened in 1883 at West Colfax and Stout streets. Farther west, Cheltenham School began classes in 1891 at West Colfax and Irving. In a short time, Denver had matched its growth of population and industry with classrooms for its children.

Professor Goldrick's efforts to educate younger citizens of Denver extended to adults as well. During the winter of 1859-1860, Goldrick and others organized The Denver City and Auraria Reading Room and Library Association. The organization had 99 members and met in meager facilities at 14th and Market streets. Although this association only lasted a few months, it demonstrated there was an interest in reading.

That same fall, another pioneer sensed the desire for reading material. Arthur E. Pierce was an unsuccessful prospector who had opened a newsstand and stationery business on a pine bench under a cottonwood tree on 11th Street in Auraria. For 50 cents a pound he had newspapers, peri-

41) The Emerson School was built in 1884 at 14th and Ogden streets. It was one of the many schools designed by noted architect Robert Roeschlaub. Today it is used as a community center.

odicals, and paper novels brought in from St. Joseph, Missouri. Business prospered, so he moved to a cabin housing Graham's Drug Store on Larimer Street between 14th and 15th. Later, with Graham as a partner, they moved to larger quarters at 15th and Larimer streets. Pierce started what could be considered Denver's first library by circulating what few books he had.

Fourteen years later, in 1874, another group of citizens formed the Denver Library Association. With a small private collection purchased from a Denver man, N. C. Bond, the Association opened its reading room on the second floor of a building at 1617 Larimer.

Again, lack of financial support plagued the library and it was forced to close in 1878. The book collection became the property of Walter Cheesman and Walter Todd, who turned the books over to the public schools with the condition that they be used to establish a free public library. The books went to the Arapahoe School, which was the high school at that time, and were made available to the public, although they did not circulate.

42) The Public Library occupied the west wing of the East Side High School from June 8, 1889, until November 1, 1899, when it consolidated with the Mercantile Library. The East Side High School was built at 19th and Stout streets in 1881. (Courtesy, Colorado Historical Society)

The library later moved to a separate wing in the new East Side High School. In 1889, John Cotton Dana was hired as librarian and the name changed to The Public Library. Dana initiated an open stack system, organized a lecture series, started study clubs and a children's library, and began a system for borrowing artwork.

While the school library was growing, a group of businessmen formed the Chamber of Commerce in 1885. Its first president, Roger Woodbury, thought that the group should sponsor a public library, reading room, and historical museum. The directors agreed, and the Mercantile Library of Denver was founded with facilities in the new Chamber of Commerce building at 14th and Lawrence streets. Always present in the affairs of Denver, pioneer Henry Brown contributed the first $1,000 to the library fund.

The Mercantile Library was successful and began receiving support from the City of Denver in 1891. Collections increased steadily, reaching more than 35,000 volumes by 1898. However, the collection outgrew the facilities of the Chamber's building. As a solution, the libraries of the Chamber of Commerce and the high school were merged in 1898 as a municipal department and became known as the Public Library of the City of Denver.

For a short time the library leased space in a two-story building at 15th and Court Place. However, the rented building did not function well as a library and was too small. An editorial in *The Denver Times* of July 11,

43) This photograph shows the loan desk at the Denver Public Library when it leased temporary space in a two-story building at 15th Street and Court Place. The library stayed here until 1903, when it moved to La Veta Place until the Carnegie Building was completed in 1910. (The Denver Public Library, Western History Department)

1901, expressed the sentiment of the day and tried to kindle some support for a new library. It called the present building "a mere shell, a flimsy firetrap, without sufficient space for either books or patrons." The editorial continued: ". . . There is certainly no one in Denver who will object to paying whatever tax may be levied for the purpose of constructing a library commensurate with the greatness of Denver as the center of culture of the mountain region." Nearly 90 years later, in 1990, Denver taxpayers voted again to allow the city to issue $91.6 million worth of bonds, of which $65 million was allocated to finance a 450,000 square foot addition to the central library.

A month after the *Times* editorial, the Board of Supervisors passed a resolution to levy a tax to provide money for site acquisition. The land ultimately selected was on Colfax and Bannock, where the original library building still stands as the only building on the Civic Center grounds. It is now used for city offices. About the same time, Andrew Carnegie made a generous donation of $200,000. With the site and the donation, Denver built its first real library and dedicated it on February 15, 1910. It occupied the building until 1956, when it moved across the Civic Center grounds to its new quarters at 14th and Broadway.

44) *The first custom-designed building for the Denver Public Library was opened in 1910. It was designed in the Greek Revival style of the Corinthian order by architect Albert Ross. When the library moved to new quarters at 14th and Broadway in 1956, the steps leading up to the main entry were removed as shown in this later photograph.*

The development of art galleries and museums did not fare as well as libraries prior to the turn of the century. For a short time, there was a small art gallery in the Castle of Culture and Commerce at the River Front Park amusement park after it first opened in 1887. The park was along the south side of the Platte between 16th and 19th streets. The so-called Art Department was run by John D. Howland, a Denver artist who was responsible for the Union Soldier sculpture in front of the State Capitol. Through the next ten years, the art room displayed various types of paintings and prints.

Downtown, the Baron Walter von Richthofen, developer of Montclair, exhibited oil paintings he had collected on his European trips. During the 1880s, they were on display at the Gettysburg Building for a 25-cent admission charge. After he displayed a nude portrait he was asked to remove his paintings, and he built his own art gallery in 1891 on the corner of Eighth and Monaco. It remained until 1901 when the building was turned into the Montclair Country Club.

For theatrical entertainment, citizens of early Denver had a better choice than they did for art. As early as 1859, two playhouses offered thespian productions. The first theater in Denver was the People's The-

45) *The Castle of Culture and Commerce was part of River Front Park, developed by John Brisben Walker in 1887. The massive stone structure was next to the 16th Street viaduct and often called Walker's Castle. The building housed displays of minerals and agricultural products as well as art. (The Denver Public Library, Western History Department)*

ater, which held performances on the second floor of the Apollo Hall, a saloon and billiard parlor. The first production, "Cross of Gold," opened on October 3, 1859. Across Cherry Creek, in Auraria, Reed's Theater was in the Cibola Hall on Ferry Street (now 11th) between Third and Fourth (Wazee and Walnut). The Cibola Minstrels opened on October 24, 1859.

A few years later, in November 1861, M. J. Dougherty, a celebrated low comedian, and J. S. Langrishe opened the Denver Theater on the corner of G Street (16th) and Lawrence. In the 1860s, other small theaters followed, including the Athenaeum on Larimer Street, the Metropolitan Theater at 15th and Cleveland Place, Walhalla Hall at 16th and Curtis, and Guards Hall at 15th and Curtis. Guards Hall later operated as the Denver Opera House.

The greatest of the theaters in early Denver was the Tabor Grand Opera House. It was built by silver king Horace Tabor and opened on September 5, 1881, at 16th and Curtis. The Tabor Grand was a magnificent structure for the time, built of red Ohio brick with white limestone trim. The interior was luxurious as well, finished with cherry wood from Japan and mahogany from Honduras and decorated with fine art from Europe. It included an elegant saloon and even had the city's first elevator. It was regarded as the finest theater in the west, and it ranked among the great theaters in the country.

Another large, elegant theater was the Broadway Theater. It was constructed in the same building as the Hotel Metropole at 18th and Broad-

46) The Tabor Grand Opera House was built in 1881 by Horace Tabor. It was one of the finest theaters of its time. It was converted to a movie theater in the 1930s and was demolished in 1964 as land was cleared for urban renewal. (The Denver Public Library, Western History Department; Photo by W. H. Jackson)

way and opened in 1890. The theater seated 1,620 patrons and also had elegant interior finishes of fine woods, ornate plaster, and painted trim. A *Seeing Denver* tour book of 1903 described it as "the leading playhouse of Denver, and during the summer months is conducted as a high-class opera house, with gardens attached."

Two other theaters built prior to the turn of the century were associated with amusement parks. When Manhattan Beach opened on the shores of Sloan's Lake on June 27, 1891, it included an auditorium that was the third largest in the United States. Most of the productions were musical comedies appropriate for summer crowds.

In May 1890, John and Mary Elitch opened their gardens at 38th and Tennyson streets. Originally purchased as a home site and garden to provide for their downtown restaurant, John and Mary Elitch decided to turn the area into a zoological garden and family resort as a way to develop a theater, which John had always wanted to do. John Elitch died shortly after the gardens opened, but Mary kept the park open. She developed the theater she and her husband had started into a stock company. For more than 100 years, it hosted some of the world's most famous actors and became the oldest continuously operating summer theater in the country. When Elitch's closed at its original location at the end of the 1994 season, the theater was still standing among the deserted amusement rides.

47) The Elitch Theater was opened in the summer of 1897 and operated continuously until Elitch's closed its north Denver location to move to the Platte Valley. It was the oldest summer stock theater in the country and hosted many great theatrical actors and actresses. (Courtesy of Elitch Gardens)

Early Denver Politics

During the boom years of the 1870s and 1880s and for several years following the depression, Denver was a wide open town. Gambling, prostitution, and bribery were common. Saloons flourished. City services such as fire and police protection were marginal, at best. The relationship between elected officials and businessmen trying to get rich was often a little too close. Denver was struggling to come to terms with its success and striving to become a great city.

Until the mid-1880s Denver was governed by a mayor and council and, in 1885, by an additional Board of Supervisors. During the last quarter of the decade, what was to become one of the most powerful political machines Denver has ever seen was slowly taking form. Its engineer was Robert Walter Speer.

Robert Speer had come to Colorado, like so many others, to alleviate his tubercular condition with the dry climate and plentiful sunshine. After he arrived in 1878, he spent time in the mountains, worked as a carpet salesman at the Daniels and Fisher department store, pursued a real estate business, and became involved in local politics.

48) *Robert Walter Speer was mayor from 1904 to 1912 and again from 1916 until his death in 1918. He was responsible for the development of the Civic Center, Speer Boulevard, and most of Denver's parkways. (The Denver Public Library, Western History Department)*

47

He was named as City Clerk in 1884 and just a year later was named by President Cleveland to be Denver's Postmaster, a position he held for four years. Speer returned to his real estate business after this job, but only until 1891.

During the time Speer was getting his start as a public servant, the citizens and state legislature recognized that politics in Denver was corrupt. In an attempt to reform city government, the state legislature created, in 1889, a Board of Commissioners of Public Works appointed by the governor, effectively taking control away from the city. In 1891, the legislature created a Fire and Police Board consisting of three members. Robert Speer was named by the governor to be on this board on which he ultimately served as president.

Although the concept of appointed commissioners was a good one, corruption continued. Employees of the police or fire department were not under any kind of civil service, so this gave the board the authority to hire and fire as it pleased. Additionally, the Fire and Police Board was responsible for licensing saloons, retail liquor stores, places of entertain-

49) Trinity Methodist Episcopal Church (now Trinity United Methodist Church) was completed in 1888, about the time Robert Speer was getting his start in politics. The church, at 18th and Broadway, was designed by Robert Roeschlaub and is considered one of his finest churches.

50) When the University of Denver moved south of the city to its present site, it hired Robert Roeschlaub to design University Hall. Constructed of volcanic lava stone, the building opened for classes in the fall of 1892.

ment, and several other types of businesses, as well as having the power to revoke permits. In all, the board could, and did, manipulate a large portion of Denver's business community. In return for political support, a somewhat tolerant attitude was taken toward such marketable vices as gambling and prostitution.

Speer served as the Police Commissioner until 1892 when Governor Waite was elected. He returned to his real estate business until being reappointed in 1897. His Democratic machine continued to grow and received an enormous boost in 1901 when the Democratic governor, James Orman, appointed Speer to be president of the Board of Public Works. The potential for political patronage in this position was greater than the previous one because Public Works controlled more than half the city's budget.

During Speer's tenure on the Public Works board, there was mounting public pressure to have Denver become a home rule city and free it from the dominance of the state legislature and the state-appointed boards. Part of the reason for this pressure was purely political rivalry between local and state factions. The other reason was probably the realization that the state boards governing the city were not effectively dealing with the problem of corruption.

51) *Before Denver became both a city and a county in 1902, the Arapahoe County Courthouse provided space for courts and county government offices on the block where the May D & F Department store was later built. The courthouse was completed in 1883, but a fourth floor was added in 1893, as this 1900 photograph shows. It was demolished in 1935 after the new City and County Building was completed. (The Denver Public Library, Western History Department)*

As a consequence of this pressure, an amendment to the state constitution was passed in 1902 which gave home rule to Denver. Several smaller municipalities—including Montclair, Globeville, Berkeley, Elyria, and Valverde—were consolidated into Denver, and the city was legally separated from Arapahoe County to become the City and County of Denver. Two years later, a city charter was adopted, which formed a strong-mayor system of city government. Under the charter, fire and police commissioners and the manager of public works were appointed by the mayor and were under the mayor's control. A further change brought about by the Constitutional amendment involved the method of granting franchises to utility corporations. The City Council previously had this power, but now all franchises had to be approved by the taxpaying electorate.

With all the changes, Speer realized that he was rapidly losing control of his machine. He was politically astute enough not to oppose the strong public sentiment favoring home rule. The only way to regain strength was to become a candidate for mayor in the first home rule election of 1904.

Robert Speer won the election, which his opponent claimed was fixed, and immediately regained power. He continued to be the traditional political boss supported by a well-greased machine and closely aligned with the business community, city service franchises, and vice. Speer is reported to have said that he would rather be called a boss than a tool without energy and friends, and that he wanted to be a good boss.

He was extremely tolerant of gambling, prostitution, and liquor interests during the first part of his term. Speer rationalized his attitude by saying that the city administration was a reflection of community ethics, and the community saw no harm in these activities. For this tolerance, however, he expected political support. He admitted graft in the city, but said that efforts were being made to keep it at a minimum. He was accused of making deals with the utility companies for their political support, and some people accused him of wanting to improve Cherry Creek and the Civic Center to enhance his own real estate holdings.

In all the controversy surrounding Mayor Speer, some of the charges were true and some were not. The record of his administration suggests that he never profited personally from his official actions, but simply wanted to improve his adopted city and maintain the power that all politicians seek to meet their objectives. He was a ruthless politician who got what he wanted with little regard to the means, but at the same time he sincerely cared about his city. He enjoyed beauty, liked animals, and sincerely wanted to make Denver a better place. His concern was to change the shape of Denver.

52) Denver had a thriving red-light district in the late 1880s and 1890s centered along Market Street between 18th and 20th streets. The house in this 1885 photo, 518 Market Street, belonged to Bella Bernard. (The Denver Public Library, Western History Department; Photo by Joseph Sturtevant Martin R. Parsons collection from Boulder Historical Society)

While Speer was building his political empire, Denver's economy, along with that of the entire state, began to crumble. The demand for silver, upon which much of the state had been built, began to level off. Railroads had been overbuilt and underfinanced. Other parts of the city and state economy were on equally shaky ground. Finally, the 1893 repeal of the Silver Purchase Act caused silver prices to plummet. Mines and smelters closed. Unemployment skyrocketed. Land developers and builders went bankrupt or had to postpone their plans. Banks closed. Denver was thrust into a severe depression.

Many of the city's wealthiest and most prominent citizens lost their fortunes in 1893. Horace Tabor lost his wealth and his mansion, as well as his opera house and business block. John Evans lost real estate. Henry Brown lost his empire. Fortunately, he completed his Brown Palace Hotel a year before the crash. It was to be his last significant building built in the struggling town where he and his wife had seen so much hope 32 years earlier. Brown spent the rest of his life fighting off creditors as a new cadre of Denverites was seeking to make fortunes and shape the city. Also in 1893, Walter Speer visited the Columbian Exposition in Chicago, a model for the design of great civic architecture throughout the country, which was to change the look of Denver from a prairie boom town to a beautiful city.

53) *Since it opened on August 12, 1892, the Brown Palace Hotel has been open for business every day and is one of Denver's best known buildings. It was built by Henry C. Brown from a design by architect Frank E. Edbrooke. The exterior is faced with Colorado red granite and Arizona sandstone.*

PART TWO

The City Beautiful: 1893 to 1930

The walk from the Brown Palace Hotel to the Civic Center is a sho‍‍rt one. There you can see a living record of Denver's history. The state capi‍‍tol anchors the east edge of this grand outdoor space on land homestead‍‍ed by Henry Brown. Water splashes in Pioneer Monument, a tribute to Denver settlers. Three library buildings from different eras embody the city's continuing belief in the importance of books and education. The outstretched arms of the City and County Building cup the west wall of the center. The tiled art museum reflects the culmination of decades of belief in the importance of culture and beauty. To the southeast, more bricks and mortar cherish the legacy of Colorado history. All around the center, buildings, monuments, and statues tell the story of Denver, from the mundane office needs of government bureaucracy to the idealistic visions of artists and planners.

1) The Pioneer monument was unveiled on June 24, 1911. Designed by French sculptor Frederick MacMonnies, the fountain commemorates Colorado pioneers. Around the rim are the figures of the prospector, the hunter, and the pioneer mother. Topping the composition is Kit Carson, looking back toward the east, but pointing the way west.

Mayor Speer and the City Beautiful

Much of what Denver is today is reflected in the Civic Center, a showcase of one of the many legacies of Mayor Walter Speer inspired by his visit to the Columbian Exposition in Chicago in 1893. The Columbian Exposition marked the birth of the "City Beautiful" movement across the country and set the style for civic improvements for several decades.

The "City Beautiful" idea was based on the three basic elements of parks, thoroughfares, and civic centers. The Chicago fair was a small-scale realization of these concepts and was designed with white buildings of classic revival style placed symmetrically around broad plazas and courts of honor. The subsequent master plans of portions of San Francisco, St. Louis, Chicago, and other cities, as well as Denver, were large-scale refinements of what was first exhibited in Chicago.

Around the turn of the century, Denver residents wanted to beautify their city and grow beyond the pioneer town image. As the city and state were recovering from the depression of 1893, the wild west boom town had been replaced by a young metropolis. Growth slowly resumed. Many people wanted to contribute to the physical improvement of the city, but there was little direction and there were no plans for organized growth.

When Walter Speer was elected mayor in 1904, Denver had the leadership and political clout to realize the "City Beautiful" concept. Speer instructed the newly formed Municipal Art Commission to hire a competent expert. They retained the services of city planner Charles Mulford Robinson, who drafted plans that included a landscaped area between the capitol, the mint, and the courthouse, which had been built in 1883 on the block bounded by 15th and 16th streets between Court Place and Tremont. However, the voters defeated a $3 million bond issue for the 1906 plan.

2) This view from the Capitol dome circa 1908 shows the area west of Broadway before the land was cleared for the Civic Center. A portion of the powerhouse for the Denver Tramway Company's cable car system is visible on the right after it was converted into shops. Farther west the library is under construction and beyond that is the U. S. Mint. (The Denver Public Library, Western History Department)

Speer revived the civic center idea and appointed an independent committee to study the situation. In August 1907, sculptor Frederick MacMonnies was in Denver to resolve problems with his design for the Pioneer Monument. He sketched a plan for his idea of a civic center, which included a large open space west of the state capitol and another building on the western edge of the open space on axis with the capitol. He also envisioned a building in the open area opposite the library, which was then under construction, to balance the composition symmetrically on either side of the east-west axis.

For the next five years, Speer worked on garnering support for the idea, working out the mechanics of assessing taxes on property in the East Denver Park District, meeting court challenges, and acquiring the property. Although there was some opposition, most Denverites supported the idea.

Real work stopped for a time in 1912 when Henry Arnold was elected mayor. Public support was too great for Arnold to abandon the civic center idea entirely, but he did have his Commissioner of Property hire famous park designer Frederick Law Olmstead, Jr., to revise the MacMonnies plan. Olmstead thought an art museum should be built to the south of the library to balance the composition, as MacMonnies had suggested. He also agreed that a large and imposing public building, strongly horizontal in design, should be built on the western end of the axis from the capitol. He said that no other buildings should be built on the site and that height restrictions on surrounding buildings should be instituted. His detailed plans for the

3) While Mayor Speer was working on his Civic Center plan, a monument commemorating the Colorado soldiers who fought and died in the Civil War was completed. Sculpted by Captain Jack Howland of the 1st Colorado Cavalry, the Civil War Memorial was unveiled on July 24, 1909.

area included a lawn with formal gardens sunken below the level of a plaza along Broadway framed on the north and south with semicircular edges. As Olmstead prepared his final plans, the area was cleared of buildings and planted as lawn during the winter of 1912-1913.

During Speer's absence, little was done. The failure to make any progress on the Civic Center was one of the things that induced Robert Speer to run for mayor again in 1916. Denverites must have been dissatisfied as well. In the same election, they voted on a charter amendment that gave back complete executive power to the mayor. It became known as the Speer Amendment and made the city's mayor one of the most powerful city administrators in the country.

4) Taken from the same position as the earlier photograph, this view shows the Civic Center around 1913 after it was cleared of buildings, but before any construction had started. Both 14th and Colfax streets continue straight through the site. (The Denver Public Library, Western History Department)

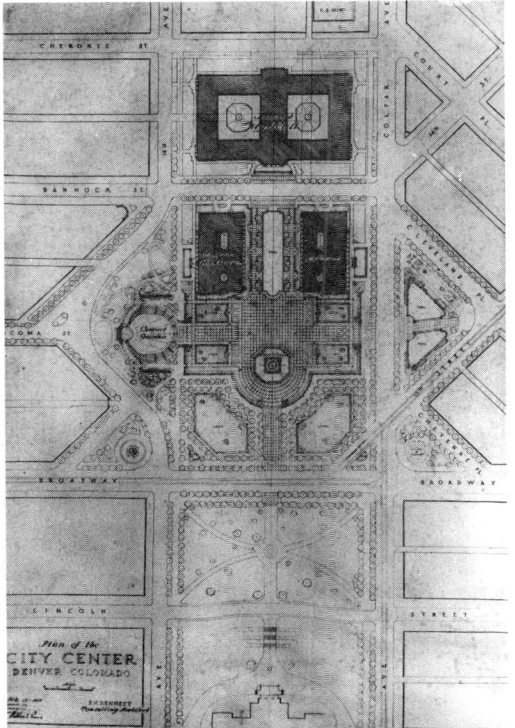

5) The 1917 E. H. Bennett plan for Civic Center showed the Greek Theater as part of the site but the triangle of land to the north was still cut off by Colfax Avenue. A city hall building is proposed across Bannock Street to the west and a new art museum is shown directly across from an expanded library building. (The Denver Public Library, Western History Department)

Once Speer was in office again, he hired Chicago architect Edward H. Bennett to design a new Civic Center. The mayor had developed some additional ideas about the project during a trip to Europe in 1911. These included creating a large meeting place for civic events, making a strong north-south axis bisecting the main east-west planning axis previous designers had suggested, and building a monument to honor the many people who had donated money or other gifts to the city. In addition to thanking the benefactors who had already given, Speer believed he could encourage more people to give if he promised them a prominent place for their names in the new Civic Center.

The Bennett plan was finalized in 1917 and showed the triangle of land to the north of Colfax as part of the composition. There was a corresponding triangle of land to the south of 14th Avenue. The north-south axis was centered on Acoma Street and included a lagoon and sculpture in the north triangle as an entrance from the downtown area. To the south was the Court of Honor to civic benefactors that mayor Speer had wanted. It surrounded a Greek theater.

Work on the Civic Center began in 1917 with construction of the four decorative pylons and line of balusters on the east side of the central open space. Although mayor Speer died unexpectedly in 1918, the Colonnade of Civic Benefactors and Greek theater were completed in 1919 and the Voorhies Memorial to the north was completed in 1922.

6) This 1922 view from the Capitol shows Civic Center when it was finally finished. Both Colfax and 14th Avenue have been rerouted. The "On the War Trail" statue across from the Bucking Bronco statue in the left center of the picture is still crated. (The Denver Public Library, Western History Department)

7) Completed in 1920, the Voorhies Memorial was provided through the bequest of John H. P. Voorhies, one of Colorado's pioneers. Architects were William E. and Arthur A. Fisher, who designed a colonnade with Ionic columns, and a high central entablature and arch opening. The pool was completed in 1922.

8) Built in conjunction with a Greek theater, the Colonnade of Civic Benefactors was Mayor Robert Speer's way of honoring citizens who gave money or other donations to the city. The names are actually on the low wall facing away from the theater rather than part of the colonnade. The panel under the pediment describes the intent.

Another Speer legacy visible today is Denver's system of parks and boulevards. Speer had begun work on his vision of an extensive park system when he was president of the Board of Public Works in 1901. However, it was not until 1907 that he had George Kessler, a leading landscape architect, draw up specs for a comprehensive plan. Kessler's vision

9) *The Greek theater in the Civic Center is surrounded by the Colonnade of Civic Benefactors and was originally used for concerts by the municipal band. To improve the acoustics, the structure was designed so that a glass "curtain" could be lowered from the superstructure behind the band. Local artist Allen True did the paintings on both sides of the stage showing two scenes of pioneer life: the trapper and the prospector. It is still used for public gatherings.*

included connecting both existing and proposed parks with an extensive citywide network of parkways. The landscaper proposed new parks at high points where people would have a clear view to the mountains.

During Speer's tenure as mayor, he doubled Denver's park space. In those parks he had the "Keep Off The Grass" signs removed, added playgrounds, built beaches and docks on the larger lakes, and included amenities like tennis courts and playing fields. Some of the open space added to Denver included Rocky Mountain Lake Park (1906); Berkeley Park (1907); Cranmer Park, originally called Mountain View Park, (1907); Sunken Gardens Park in front of West High School (1907); and Arlington Park (1911). In addition, land for Inspiration Point in northwest Denver was purchased in 1909, some acreage around Sloan's Lake was acquired in 1906, and Washington Park was extended to the south and included the newly dredged Grasmere Lake.

Some of the boulevards were never completed, but today's parkways of Sixth Avenue, Seventh Avenue, 17th Avenue, and Montview Boulevard

10) The "On The War Trail" statue was erected in May 1922 and depicts an Indian brandishing a lance in defiance of the conquering white man. The monument was donated by Stephen Knight, who was prompted to give $16,500 to the city after Mayor Speer announced that people who donated would have their names inscribed on the Colonnade of Civic Benefactors.

are from the Speer era, as are Monaco Boulevard, Marion Street Parkway, the Williams Street Parkway, the Cheesman Park Esplanade, and several others scattered around the city. Some of the tree-lined streets, like Federal Boulevard and Colorado Boulevard, lost their stately trees when space for automobiles became more important than landscaped parkways.

The most well-known parkway is Speer Boulevard, renamed from Cherry Creek Drive by the City Council in 1910. Prior to Mayor Speer's involvement, Cherry Creek had been a shallow, meandering creek, often nearly devoid of water. During heavy rains it was prone to flooding and served as little more than an open sewer and dumping place. In 1907, Speer began the channelization of the creek to improve flood control and lined the higher portion of the banks with trees, streetlights, and sidewalks. Today, Speer Boulevard has been renovated with new landscaping and streetlights similar to those originally used. A bicycle trail and footpath have been added at creek level.

11) Speer Boulevard runs along both sides of Cherry Creek, which Mayor Speer had channelized around 1910. Today, the landscaped path along the river is a popular spot for hikers and bicycle riders.

Speer was also instrumental in getting the City Auditorium built. Once late-19th century conventioneers discovered Denver, the city needed a hall to accommodate large groups. Financed with a voter-approved bond issue, the auditorium was built on 14th between Curtis and Champa streets. It was completed in 1908 and hosted the Democratic National Convention that year.

The architect, Robert Willison, designed the structure so that it could be converted, with a system of movable walls, from a 3,300-seat theater into a 12,000-capacity convention hall. It also contained a pipe organ. At the time it was built, it was the second-largest municipal auditorium in the country. After an adjoining arena was opened in 1952, the auditorium was converted into a theater that was home to the Denver Symphony Orchestra as well as touring theater productions. A 1993 remodeling restored much of the auditorium's exterior appearance.

12) This 1930 photograph of the old City Auditorium, completed in 1908 during Mayor Speer's administration, is now part of the Denver Center for the Performing Arts. It houses a 2,170-seat theater as well as meeting rooms for the adjacent Currigan Hall. (Courtesy of Denver Theaters and Arenas)

Although the Civic Center, the parks and parkway system, and the City Auditorium were Mayor Speer's most visible accomplishments, he was responsible for many other improvements to the city. Between 1905 and 1912, the city gave away more than 110,000 elm and maple saplings to people who would plant them. Many of today's mature trees are a result of Speer's efforts. On the practical side, he built storm and sanitary sewers, graded and paved more than 300 miles of streets, had downtown telephone and telegraph lines buried, and lit the roadways with new street lamps. This was a practical as well as an aesthetic improvement: Since 1883, the center of the city had been illuminated by the harsh glare of arc lights on 150-foot high towers.

Despite the corruption and political muscle exerted by Robert Speer, he truly loved Denver and contributed as much as any mayor or private citizen to giving it much of the form it has today.

13) *The Voorhies Memorial completed the north end of the Civic Center design. The planners had always envisioned a structure that would act as a gateway or link to the rest of the downtown area. The classic Ionic design provides a historic contrast to contemporary construction.*

Growth After the 1893 Depression

After the crash of 1893, Denver learned not to stake its future on mining alone. Even though the discovery of gold around Cripple Creek in 1891 and its subsequent mining helped Denver recover from the depression, it needed a more diversified economy to maintain its place as Queen City of the Plains.

Longtime residents and newcomers alike tried new enterprises to make their fortunes just as the early pioneers had done with mining. Ranching and farming continued to grow as they had in the 1880s, and Denver became the regional center for meat processing plants, flour mills, dairies, and other food processing businesses. Oil and coal production in the region benefited the city as did new manufacturing plants. The tourism industry expanded as more people around the country discovered Colorado. Even disease brought thousands of people to Denver when tuberculosis sufferers flooded in to seek relief in the dry, mile-high atmosphere.

14) The Monarch Mills Building at 1495 Delgany Street was Denver's last surviving flour mill. It was built shortly after the turn of the century as part of the city's growing role as an agricultural processing center. A fire on December 30, 1993, destroyed all but the six-story grain elevator.

Between the depression of 1893 and the stock market crash of 1929, commercial and industrial areas expanded. Downtown, a thriving warehouse district developed along Wynkoop and Blake Streets. Among the many storehouses was the C. S. Morey Mercantile Building, constructed in 1896 at 16th and Wynkoop. It was soon followed with stoutly constructed brick and timber edifices like the J. S. Brown Mercantile Building at 18th and Wynkoop in 1899 and the Spratlen-Anderson Mercantile at 1450 Wynkoop in 1910. The Littleton Creamery-Beatrice Foods Warehouse was built in 1903, and today has been renovated as the Denver Design Center, a collection of showrooms for the interior design trade.

Sixteenth Street developed as Denver's first shopping strip. One of the most prominent structures built during this period was the Daniels & Fisher store and its attached clock tower. The business was originally opened in 1864 by William B. Daniels and J. M. Eckart as a small dry goods store at 15th and Larimer streets. Later, Eckart sold his interest to William M. Fisher and they opened a small store at 16th and Lawrence

15) *The Denver Design Center at the Ice House was originally a refrigerated warehouse. The massive brick structure was built in 1903 and later served as the headquarters for the Beatrice Creamery after it purchased the Littleton Creamery in 1912. It was remodeled in 1986 for the Design Center.*

streets in 1875. As business grew, the store was rebuilt and expanded. William Daniels' son, William Cooke Daniels, became sole owner of the store with the death of Fisher in 1897. He wanted to build the finest store in the area and give Denver a landmark.

Daniels built his shopping emporium at the corner of 16th and Arapahoe streets with the tower modeled after the Campanile of St. Marks in Venice. The store was completed in 1912 and was the tallest structure in Denver until 1956, when the Mile High Center was constructed at 17th and Broadway. The Daniels & Fisher Store was sold to the May Company and became the May-D&F Store when it moved to 16th and Tremont in 1958. It was later sold to Foley's, and the downtown store closed in 1993. The main portion of the Daniels & Fisher store was demolished in 1971 as part of the Skyline Urban Renewal Project, but the tower was saved and converted into 1,000-square-foot offices on each floor of the 40-foot square structure. The new brick on the northwest and northeast sides indicates where the old structure abutted the tower.

16) Before the main portion of the building was demolished in February 1971, the Daniels and Fisher store stretched the entire length of 16th Street between Lawrence and Arapahoe. When it was completed in 1912, it was one of Denver's most popular stores. (The Denver Public Library, Western History Department)

Another venerable Denver institution was the Denver Dry Goods Company. The store began in 1886 as the McNamara Dry Goods Company at 15th and Larimer. A three-story building was constructed at 16th and California in 1889. When the 1893 panic forced the owners to surrender the store to bankers Dennis Sheedy and Charles Kountze, the store was renamed the Denver Dry Goods Company. Business was so good that a fourth floor was added in 1900 and a fifth floor in 1924. An additional six-story building was constructed on the 15th Street side in 1905. The Denver Dry remained one of the city's finest department stores until 1986, when it was sold to the May Company. The store was closed in 1987 and remained vacant until 1993, when the building was remodeled and converted into condominiums and retail stores.

Across California Street, Meyer and Max Neusteter opened a women's store in 1911. In 1924, the store was expanded and the current building constructed. It, too, was one the finest stores in Denver until it closed in 1986. Like the Denver Dry, it has been converted into condominiums on the upper floors with shops at street level. Other stores—like Gano-Downs, Joslin's, and Cottrell's—also favored 16th Street, making it a favorite spot for Saturday shopping excursions until outlying shopping centers began to attract the attention of shoppers in the late 1950s and 1960s.

17) This view along 17th Street toward the northwest shows the cable car tracks of the Denver City Cable Railway company and its smoking stack at the right of the picture. The tall building on the left is the Equitable Building. At this time there were still single-family houses along Welton Street in the foreground. (Courtesy of Denver Water Department)

After the panic of 1893, office buildings were built as fast as stores. The buildings still standing include the Symes Building on the southwest corner of 16th and Champa (1905) and the Ideal Building at 17th and Champa (1907). The Ideal Building was expanded in 1927 to house the Denver National Bank and was restored in 1980 for Colorado Savings and Loan.

Other buildings included the Denver Gas and Electric Building, built in 1910 at 15th and Champa with Frank Edbrooke as the architect. It was later renamed the Insurance Exchange Building and still sports its magnificent bank of light bulbs built into the facade. Also on Champa and 16th Street across from the Symes Building is the University Building. This structure was built in 1911 and was originally called the A. C. Foster Building until it was purchased by the University of Denver.

18) The 12-story University Building at 16th and Champa streets is an elegant design of granite, brick, and terracotta. It was one of the first buildings built after a 1908 ordinance allowing such tall structures. An earlier 1904 city ordinance had limited building heights to 125 feet or nine stories.

To house the growing demand for government office space as a result of World War I, the State Office Building on the northeast corner of Colfax and Sherman was completed in 1921. On the other side of the Capitol, at 14th and Sherman, the Colorado State Museum, designed by Frank Edbrooke, opened in 1915. These two buildings added to the concentration of government and cultural buildings around the Civic Center. The State Office Building was renovated in 1985 and has one of the most elegant lobbies of any government building in the city. After the museum moved to its present location at 13th and Broadway in 1976, the old museum building was renovated for state offices and reopened on November 21, 1986.

19) Although ornate by today's standards, the State Office Building showed the tendency toward designing strictly functional accommodations for governmental office needs when it was completed in 1921. The building was designed in the classical revival style of Roman Corinthian by architect William E. Bowman.

20) The original Colorado State Museum was built in 1915 to house the ever-growing collections of the Colorado State Historical Society, which prior to that time was situated in the basement of the Capitol. It was constructed of granite from Cotopaxi, Colorado, with interior finishes of Colorado yule marble.

Denver's banking houses also expanded after the depression to meet the needs of a growing city. From its humble beginnings as the Clark, Gruber & Company, the First National Bank built its first building at 15th and Blake in 1865, but later moved to 17th Street as most of the banks did. In 1911, it moved to a new 12-story building at 17th and Stout, and now is being rehabilitated into a hotel.

The other longtime Denver Bank, Colorado National, moved to its present location in 1915. An addition was made along Champa Street in 1926, which doubled its size and exactly matched the original building. Additional floors were added in the 1960s, and the tower at 17th and Curtis was completed in 1973.

Two banks that opened after the 1893 panic were Central Bank and Trust and United States National Bank. Central Bank started as North Side Bank in 1892, but opened its headquarters at 15th and Arapahoe streets in 1911. A longtime officer of the bank, Elwood Brooks, was honored by having the Brooks Towers apartments named after him. The bank helped develop the project in the mid-1960s on the site of the former Mining Exchange Building. The statue of the miner that stood on top of the building now graces the entry to the new building as a reminder of Denver's past. Central Bank moved to the Park Central Building, a sleek, new office building across 15th Street, in 1973. The original Central Bank Building was demolished in 1990 after the bank was acquired by First Bank of Minneapolis.

21) Colorado National Bank has been at its present location since 1915. The neoclassical building was enlarged in 1926 and the current modern addition placed on top of the original structure in 1964.

22) *The heavy stonework of the Mining Exchange Building anchored the corner of 15th and Arapahoe streets when it was built in 1891. A statue of a miner was saved when the building was demolished in 1963 for the Brooks Towers Apartment. The miner now stands in front of the entrance. (Courtesy, Colorado Historical Society)*

United States National Bank opened its doors in 1904 in the Ernest & Cranmer Building. It moved into the U. S. National Bank Building in 1921 and later built its own building at 17th and Stout. In 1956, it moved to the Mile High Center on Broadway designed by I. M. Pei, and merged with the Denver National Bank in 1959 to become the Denver United States National Bank. The name was later changed to United Bank of Denver and is today Norwest Bank.

The federal government joined with private bankers in maintaining an interest in Denver as a financial center. Although Congress had passed a law in 1862 creating a U. S. Mint in Denver and had purchased the facilities of Clark, Gruber & Company, the mint only served as an assay office. In 1895, Congress passed acts establishing a mint at Denver for the coinage of gold and silver, and for purchasing a site and funding a new building.

The government found a site near the future Civic Center on Colfax between Cherokee and Delaware streets. Construction was completed in 1904, but actual minting did not begin until 1906. Additions to the original building were made in 1936, 1946, 1965, and 1990.

The original building was modeled after the Italian Renaissance style and strongly resembles the Palazzo Riccardi in Florence, Italy. The lower portion of the building was faced with Colorado granite and the upper portion with

23) The original structure of the U. S. Mint dates from 1904 and still stamps out millions of coins each year. In the lobby of the first floor are mural paintings depicting mining, agriculture, and manufacturing executed by artist Edwin H. Blashfield, assisted by his pupil, Vincente Adriente.

granite from Maine. The foundation was constructed with more than one million bricks, and the exterior walls were made three feet thick. Interior corridors were handsomely finished with gray-veined white Vermont marble using Tennessee marble for door and window trim.

Outside of Denver, agriculture flourished after 1900 and had a direct impact on the city. Tens of thousands of people started farms in the early part of the century, and livestock, including cattle and sheep, were herded into the ever-expanding packing houses north of the city. From the earliest days, people recognized the potential of Colorado for farming and ranching.

Denver's first stockyard opened in 1865 and was known as the Bull's Head Corral. The Denver Union Stockyards were located at their present site in 1881 and grew steadily after that. To conduct the business of the industry, The Livestock Exchange Building at 47th and Lafayette was completed in 1916.

24) The Livestock Exchange Building was built in 1916 after the Denver Union Stockyards were located at their present site. The building is still used today.

To promote the industry, The National Stockgrowers Association included an exhibition of range cattle in 1899 as part of its annual meeting. From this, the association developed the exhibit into the Western Livestock Show, which first opened in January 1906. A tent was first used for the show, but later a large pavilion was built, which is still in use. Today, the two-week long National Western Stock Show is still held in January and is the largest such show in the country combining stock exhibitions, auctions, vendor booths, and a daily rodeo. Attendance in 1994 reached 527,606. Several buildings make up the complex, including the 1952 Denver Coliseum and a new $10.5 million Events Center completed in 1994 as part of a $30 million bond issue passed in 1989 for upgrading the stock show facilities.

While Denverites worked to recover from the 1893 panic, they also had time to play and develop the cultural institutions that would continue into the next century. To celebrate the renewed hope brought about by the new gold discoveries around Cripple Creek and the ever-increasing farm prosperity, the Chamber of Commerce organized the Festival of Mountain and Plain in October 1895. The festival included parades, Indian dancers, horse shows, fireworks, rodeos, band contests, miner's rock drill contests, and a host of similar activities. It was a Mardi Gras-like atmosphere, and by the turn of the century it was one of the major events in the city as well as a tourist attraction. Organizers presented the Mountain and Plain festival yearly from 1895 to 1915, missing only a few years. Many of the activities were held in a large outdoor stadium built on the northeast corner of Colfax and Broadway.

25) *Colfax and Broadway was the site of the Festival of Mountain and Plain at the turn of the century. Temporary grandstands were constructed for the shows. The yearly event continues today in the Civic Center Park as the "Taste of Colorado." (Courtesy, Colorado Historical Society)*

The idea was revived in 1972 as an arts and crafts show to raise funds for the Library Associates of Colorado Women's College. It gradually expanded and became a broader-based festival and was held in various locations around the city.

The Festival of Mountain and Plain was only one of Denver's many tourist attractions. As today, the recreational opportunities and beauty of the mountains as well as Colorado's climate lured visitors from around the country. Tourism began with the arrival of the first railroad, but steadily increased throughout the early part of the century. After the invention of the automobile, touring became popular around the country in the 1920s. To promote the city to car-driving visitors, the city established camps in some of the local parks where people could find a place to park their car, camp, and shower.

Amusement parks also provided recreational diversions. Although they were not amusement parks in today's sense of the word, Denver had several play areas beginning as early as 1866 with Ford Park near 36th and Race streets. River Front Park, along the South Platte River between 15th and 19th streets, was popular in the 1880s and 1890s. Baron von Richthofen's Sans Souci Gardens on South Broadway also was popular for a few years in the early 1880s as was Arlington Park at Fourth and Corona. Arlington Park was later called Chutes Park after the attraction in which visitors could ride small boats down a chute into a small lake.

26) For 17 years after its opening in 1891, Manhattan Beach was a popular Denver attraction on the shores of Sloan's Lake. No alcohol was allowed, so people slipped out through the fence to cross the county line (Sheridan Boulevard) to Edgewater where saloons, gambling, and the local red light district were easily accessible. (The Denver Public Library, Western History Department)

In 1891 Manhattan Beach opened along the northwest shore of Sloan's Lake. The park included zoo animals, a large theater, beaches, promenades, a roller coaster, and other amusement park rides, and a boat called the "City of Denver," which gave rides to as many as 150 people at a time. Manhattan Beach was a popular attraction until a fire destroyed it in 1908. It was reopened as Luna Park in 1909, but never regained popularity.

The year Manhattan Beach burned, Lakeside Amusement Park opened. Located along Sheridan Boulevard at 46th Avenue, Lakeside was known as White City because its entrance tower and large buildings were painted white. The park sported the usual amusement rides along with a large pavilion for dancing and a theater. While many of the original buildings have been demolished, the tower remains and Lakeside thrives today in the same location where the roller coaster and other rides are popular attractions for the latest generation of thrill-seekers.

27) *Originally billed as the Coney Island of the West, Lakeside Amusement Park opened in 1908. The large dance hall, indoor swimming pool, and many of the white wooden buildings are gone now, but the lighted entry tower at right remains at its location near Inspiration Point. (The Denver Public Library, Western History Department; Photo by McClure)*

Perhaps the best known Denver amusement park for more than 100 years is Elitch's. Opened in 1890 by John and Mary Elitch as gardens, a small zoo, and a theater, Elitch's soon became a popular destination for Denverites who rode the trolley cars to the gate at West 38th and Tennyson. In the early years, Elitch's offered picnic areas, pony rides, a miniature train, playgrounds, zoo animals, entertainers, and the famous Elitch theater which became the oldest continuously operating summer theater in the country. As the park matured, more amusement rides were built, supplanting many of the gardens and picnic areas.

In the early 1920s, Elitch's built the Trocadero Ballroom. This was a 15,000-square-foot dance floor surrounded by seating areas where the weary dancers could rest between spins on the floor. It was open on the

28) Elitch's Amusement Park was located in North Denver at 38th Avenue and Tennyson streets for more than 100 years. For generations of Denverites, Elitch's meant excitement, rides, romance, and beautifully maintained flower beds. It moved to the Platte Valley in 1995 after outgrowing its original site. (Courtesy of Elitch Gardens)

29) The big band sound was common at the Trocadero Ballroom at Elitch's during the '20s, '30s, and '40s. It was a favorite spot for visitors and residents alike, but was razed in 1975 after years of declining popularity. (Courtesy of Elitch Gardens)

sides, so the sounds of the big bands permeated the surrounding park. For more than 50 years, the Trocadero hosted the most famous bands in the country and was one of Denver's most romantic meeting places. Succumbing to economic pressures and the fading of big band popularity, the Trocadero was demolished in 1975.

Constrained by the surrounding neighborhood in what once had been farmland, Elitch's moved to a larger site in the Platte Valley in 1995. Here it continues the tradition of wholesome, family-oriented entertainment for the city and maintains the slogan, "Not to see Elitch's is not to see Denver."

When the amusement parks were closed, Denverites could visit one of the many theaters in the city. After the first movie was shown at Elitch's theater in 1896 using Thomas Edison's Vitascope, show houses began to spring up around town. At first, most of the theaters showed live performances. The Denham hosted Shakespeare, the Curtis showed melodrama, and the Orpheum was a vaudeville house. Many of the theaters were downtown on Curtis Street. Because of the thousands of electric lights that illuminated the theaters, Curtis became known as Denver's Great White Way.

30) *The theaters on Curtis Street, Denver's "Great White Way," provided a variety of entertainment in the first part of the century. (Courtesy, Colorado Historical Society)*

As motion pictures became more popular, many of the early auditoriums eventually were turned into movie theaters. Beginning in the 1920s, several theaters specially built for movies were constructed, including the Denver Theater at 16th and Glenarm in 1928, the Aladdin on East Colfax in 1927, and the Center on 16th near Court Place in 1954. Most of the grand theaters of the era were built around a theme, like the Mayan on South Broadway or the Oriental in North Denver. The exterior design and interior decoration of these movie palaces reflected their themes and added to the fantasy of going to the movies.

The only remaining grand theater from the era is the Art Deco-inspired Paramount, built in 1929 at 16th and Glenarm Place. The 16th Street entrance, brightly lit marquee, and grand staircase were demol-

31) The Mayan Theater on South Broadway is one of the last remaining thematic theaters in the city. Harry E. Huffman built and owned many of Denver's best-known theaters during the first half of the century.

ished in 1985 during a renovation of the Kittredge Building, but the grand interior with its Wurlitzer organ still remains. The entrance to the theater, designed by architect Temple Buell, is now on Glenarm. Financial problems plagued the theater in the early 1990s, and its future remained uncertain after it was ordered into receivership in April 1994.

For more cultural entertainment, residents of the growing metropolis also enjoyed a developing art museum in the early part of the century. The first organized effort to establish an art program for the city occurred in 1893 when the Denver Artists Club was founded. The club was restricted to "elected, qualifying artists" and met in each others' studios, hired models for group painting sessions, discussed art, and once a year sponsored a public exhibit.

When the club changed its name in 1917 to the Denver Art Association, it dropped the requirement that all members be artists. For several years, the association housed what collections it had in various locations including the public library and the Museum of Natural History in City Park.

32) The Colorado Museum of Natural History was built in 1908 to house the collection of pioneer naturalist Professor Edwin Carter. This mid-1930s photograph shows the wing on the left, which was completed in 1918, and the 1929 William H. James Memorial Hall on the right. The windows were bricked to provide more space for exhibits. (Courtesy of Colorado State Archives)

In 1920, the association hired its first full-time director, George William Eggers of Chicago. One of his first acts was to change the name of the organization to the Denver Art Museum. In 1922, the museum found its first permanent home when the Chappell House at 13th and Logan was donated by Mrs. George Cranmer, wife of a prominent Denver civic leader, and her brother Delos Chappell.

By 1924, Mayor Benjamin Stapleton expressed city interest in establishing a museum and wanted it to be located somewhere near the Civic Center. The city gave the museum $3,000 in 1925 and allotted exhibition space on the fourth floor in the newly completed City and County Building in 1932. Chappell House continued to house temporary exhibitions and the expanding American Indian collection until it was razed in 1970.

The museum operated as the art agency of the city for two years and enjoyed annual appropriations for operation and maintenance. In July 1934, the City Council made the museum a permanent department of the City and County of Denver.

33) *Chappell House was the first permanent home of the Denver Art Museum when it was donated to the institution. It housed part of the collection until 1970, when it was torn down. (Courtesy of Denver Art Museum)*

The Expanding City

The panic of 1893 had the immediate effect of slowing Denver's booming population, which had exploded threefold during the 1880s. By 1890, the city's population count stood at 106,713. Once the effects of the depression subsided and the economy diversified into areas other than mining, Denver's population began to grow again, jumping nearly 80,000 in the ten years prior to 1910 when it reached 213,331. By 1930, 287,861 people lived in the city of Denver and another 64,702 in Adams, Arapahoe, and Jefferson counties.

To accommodate this growth, neighborhoods expanded beyond the core city and roads, bridges, utilities, and other city services grew with them. As part of Mayor Speer's City Beautiful dream, parks and parkways were acquired and grew with the neighborhoods, sometimes preceding them. Schools, churches, libraries, and other institutions also were built to keep pace with the city's growth.

Most of the growth of residential neighborhoods after the turn of the century radiated from the fringes of existing neighborhoods near the downtown area. Areas like Highlands, Berkeley, Sloan's Lake, Globeville, Cheesman Park, Park Hill, Montclair, Washington Park, and South Denver sprouted dozens of housing developments.

34) *The typical Denver bungalow style of house can be found in nearly all of the older neighborhoods in the city. In most cases, bungalows were squeezed onto the narrow lots that were typical of residential development after the turn of the century.*

Most Denverites lived in three basic housing styles: the Denver square, the bungalow, and the cottage. The Denver square was built by developers after the depression of 1893 into the 1920s. It was similar to the foursquare houses being built elsewhere in the country and consisted of a rectangular, two-story brick structure with attached wooden front and back porches. Variations on the basic design included brick porches, an occasional bay window, Neoclassical or Colonial Revival ornamentation, or other decorative touches.

The bungalow style house was used frequently from the early part of the century into the 1930s. It, too, had a simple, rectangular plan and was typically constructed of brick, but was usually only one story high. The bungalows had gabled roofs and front and back porches of either wood or brick. Exposed beams around the front porch and elsewhere reflected the more elaborate bungalow style started by the Green Brothers in California.

The classic cottage style was the third common type of Denver house built around the turn of the century. It is similar to the bungalow style with a rectangular plan and attached front and back porches. The primary brick structure was often built on a raised stone foundation.

All of the older Denver neighborhoods display these three basic housing styles and their variations, occasionally interrupted with an old farm house or other residence predating 1890.

35) *The Zang Mansion was built by Adolph Zang in 1905. The Neoclassical style house is representative of the many fine mansions that still stand on Capitol Hill. Adolph Zang was active in banking and insurance as well as brewing. He was the son of Philip Zang, founder of the largest pre-prohibition brewery in the Rockies. The elegant interior finishes have been preserved, and the structure is now used for offices.*

Above: Every summer, the downtown office buildings provide a backdrop for the brilliant flower beds in Civic Center Park.

Left: The Denver Botanic Gardens sit on the site of a former graveyard. In addition to the extensive outdoor gardens, the Boettcher Conservatory provides a home for tropical plants in Denver's arid climate.

Left: *Colorado sandstone frames the Cherry Creek Bike Trail as it passes near the Cherry Creek Shopping Center. Denver has an extensive system of bike trails.*

Right: *Writer's Square is a full-block mixed-use development of offices, shops, and condominiums. Its plazas provide a convenient pedestrian connection between Larimer Square and the 16th Street Mall.*

Left: *The fabric roof of the main terminal of Denver International Airport glows at night from the lights inside. Outlying terminals are reached by underground trains. (Courtesy of Denver International Airport)*

Right: *Above the entrances to the stage of the Greek Theater in Civic Center are two murals painted by Denver artist Allen True. The murals, painted in 1920, depict the figures of the trapper and the prospector, which represent the early pioneers in Colorado. The fading paintings were restored in 1976.*

Left: *The multi-faceted walls of the Denver Art Museum glisten in an infinite number of ways as the light changes. Italian Architect Gio Ponti was fascinated with the quality of Denver's light and had the Corning Glass Company develop special tiles that would withstand the city's climate. More than one million tiles were hand placed.*

Right: *The visitor's gallery in the Capitol dome offers a panoramic view of the Civic Center, downtown Denver, the eastern plains, and the Rocky Mountains.*

Above: Except for four years during World War II, the City and County Building has been decorated every Christmas since 1935 with lights and displays. The tradition started in 1919 when the city began to decorate and light structures in Civic Center Park.

Below: The 16th Street Mall is a popular place for noontime crowds. Outdoor cafes and seating areas line the mall where people can take a free shuttle from one end to the other.

Right: *Most of the buildings in Larimer Square date from the late 19th century and have been renovated into shops and offices. Larimer Square is a mecca for residents and tourists alike along what General William Larimer called in 1858 "the best" street.*

Below: *Fillmore Plaza leads from First Avenue to Second Avenue into the Cherry Creek North shopping area. The district includes a diverse collection of small upscale shops, restaurants, and offices.*

Right: *The Cherry Creek Shopping Center is one of Denver's most popular retail centers. High-quality stores and a well-designed mall have made it a destination point. The 130-store mall was rated Colorado's number one tourist attraction for 1991-92 by the Denver Metro Convention and Visitors Bureau.*

Right: *Every football season, Bronco mania takes over. The Denver Broncos play in Mile High Stadium to sold-out crowds every game. (Courtesy of Denver Broncos Football Club, Photo by Eric Lars Bakke)*

Left: *After decades of waiting, Denver finally got its major league baseball team in 1993, the Colorado Rockies. For the first two years the team played in Mile High Stadium while Coors Field was being constructed in lower downtown. The team's 1995 season opened in the new venue. (Courtesy of Rich Clarkson & Associates, Photo by Emmett Jordan)*

Below: *The Denver Parks and Recreation Department does a magnificent job every year planting the parks and parkways with flowers. One of the most elaborate plantings is done on the west side of Washington Park.*

Left: *The beauty of the State Capitol and Civic Center stand as legacies to Henry C. Brown and Mayor Robert Speer. Brown donated part of his homestead to the state in 1868 for the Capitol building to help increase the property values of his adjacent land. Speer created the Civic Center.*

Lower left: *In recent years, brew pubs have become a popular business. In mid-1994, there were 42 brew pubs and microbreweries in Colorado. With microbreweries and giants like Coors and Anheuser-Busch, more beer is produced in Colorado than in any other state. The Rock Bottom Brewery serves outdoor diners in the shadow of the Daniels and Fisher tower along the 16th Street Mall.*

Lower right: *The Brown Palace was one of the first hotels planned around an open atrium. It was the second fireproof building in the United States, and much of the interior is finished with onyx from Mexico. It has been host to countless visitors since it opened in 1892. Presidents, movie stars, and even The Beatles have stayed at the Brown.*

Above: *The galleria of the Denver Center for the Performing Arts provides a covered outdoor promenade connecting the remodeled City Auditorium with the newer structures. The center is the second-largest performing arts complex in the country after Lincoln Center in New York. (Courtesy of Denver Theaters and Arenas, Photo by Krebs Uptown Photography)*

Below: *The west side of the Museum of Natural History provides a sweeping view of City Park Lake, the Pavilion, downtown Denver, and the mountains. The entry to the museum used to be on the west side, but was moved to the north side when major additions were made in 1987.*

Left: The Capitol dome is covered with real gold leaf. The idea of using gold was both symbolic and practical. It represents the commodity that pioneers sought when they founded Denver and Colorado, and it was deemed a more suitable roofing material than the bronze paints and lacquer-covered copper the builders originally tried.

Below: The interior of the Capitol dome rises 180 feet above the grand staircase leading to the second floor. Near the top of the dome are 16 stained-glass portraits of pioneers who helped in the early development of the state.

Below: The Colonnade of Civic Benefactors was Mayor Robert Speer's way of encouraging citizens to donate to the city in the early part of the century. The names of the early givers and a few recent additions can be found on the east side of the east wall surrounding the Greek Theater in Civic Center, somewhat obscured by overgrown plants.

Right: *The classical design of the Civic Center, including its balustrades and decorative pylons, was inspired by the Columbian Exposition held in Chicago in 1893. A much-needed restoration of Civic Center was completed in 1991.*

Above: *The Tivoli Brewery was established in 1860 by John Good, who bought an established brewery, enlarged it, and named it after the Tivoli Gardens in Copenhagen. It produced beer until 1969. After sitting vacant for many years, it was remodeled into a collection of shops, restaurants, and movie theaters in 1985. The flagging development was purchased by the Auraria Higher Education Complex and was converted into a new student, food, and retail center in 1994.*

Right: *Elitch Gardens has been a popular Denver attraction since 1890. The Ferris wheel was a popular ride at the park's original location in north Denver through the 1994 season, a year before Elitch's relocated to the Platte Valley.*

Left: *One of the names on the Colonnade of Civic Benefactors is Joseph A. Thatcher. He was honored after he donated $100,000 for this monument and fountain at the north end of the City Park Esplanade.*

Below: *The Taste of Colorado/Festival of Mountain and Plain, held in the Civic Center during the Labor Day weekend, is the descendant of the original Festival of Mountain and Plain. The festival began in 1895 as a way to celebrate the renewed prosperity of mining and agriculture after the 1893 depression.*

Left: Octoberfest is held in Larimer Square every fall. The festival includes bands, street performers, food booths, and plenty of beer.

Below: Golfers at Willis Case municipal golf course have a spectacular view from the clubhouse and first tee. The course was developed from nine holes acquired from the failed Interlachen Country Club in 1929 and from a nine-hole course originally built by the Shriners on the north side of the ridge.

Below: The central business district lies at a lower elevation than the rest of Denver, giving players at City Park Golf Course a view of fall colors, the skyline, and early autumn snow in the mountains.

Left: The 2,900-seat Temple Hoyne Buell Theater hosts Broadway shows and other large productions. A completely new theater was built within the shell of the old auditorium arena. The theater opened in 1991 and features a stage that is 55 feet deep and 123 feet wide. (Courtesy of Denver Theaters and Arenas, Photo by Krebs Uptown Photography)

Below: The Tattered Cover Bookstore is one of Denver's treasures. Started by Joyce Meskis in 1974, it is now the largest independent bookstore in the United States with more than 400,000 books on four floors. A well-read, helpful staff and cozy reading chairs greet customers.

Above: *This is the architect's drawing of the south elevation of the Central Library. The first phase of the 540,000-square-foot building was scheduled to open in March 1995. (Courtesy of Klipp Colussy Jenks DuBois Architects and the Denver Public Library)*

Left: *United Bank of Denver modified the Mile High Center in the mid-1980s with the addition of an atrium space attached to the original office tower and a 50-story tower on corner of 17th Street and Lincoln. United Bank merged with Norwest Corporation of Minneapolis in 1991, and the name was changed to Norwest Bank in 1992.*

Left: *The Children's Museum was founded in 1975 and for nine years operated in a rented storefront. This colorful structure was built for the museum in 1984 next to the Platte River across I-25 from Mile High Stadium.*

Left: The Creekfront plaza and park where Larimer Street crosses Cherry Creek is a popular respite for downtown workers and students from the Auraria Higher Education Complex. The artwork, called "Petros" by artist Bill Gian, was completed in 1992.

Above: Red Rocks amphitheater was built between two huge natural rock outcroppings during the Depression. The natural sidewalls and large rock behind the stage provide excellent acoustics. Visitors sitting in the upper seats have magnificent views of the city lights and the rising moon during evening concerts. Easter sunrise services are held here every year. (Courtesy of Denver Theaters and Arenas, Photo by Krebs Uptown Photography)

On next page: The view from Highlands is much different today than it was when General William Larimer forded the South Platte River to lay out the town of Highland in 1858 after he founded Denver.

For the wealthy, custom-designed houses and mansions were the rule. After the turn of the century, the well-to-do built farther away from the Capitol Hill area in neighborhoods like Cheesman Park, the Polo Club, and around the Denver Country Club. Many of the mansions were designed in the Neoclassical style, but Colonial Revival, Spanish Revival, English Revival, and many other styles also were popular. Today, many of the larger, custom-designed mansions sit side by side with developer houses that came after them.

To provide for the spiritual needs of the growing population, churches were built as fast as houses. For the Jewish community, the second Temple Emanuel was built at 16th and Pearl streets in 1899. It replaced the first Temple Emanuel that had occupied the corner of 19th and Curtis since 1874. In north Denver, Mount Carmel Church was built on Navajo Street in 1904 and St. Patrick's Catholic Church at 33rd and Pecos streets in 1907.

36) The stately Grant-Humphreys mansion sits high on Capitol Hill with a grand view of the Rocky Mountains. It was built in 1902 by James B. Grant, founder of the Grant smelter and a former governor. It was purchased in 1917 by Albert E. Humphreys, who made his fortune in oil. The house was donated to the Colorado Historical Society in 1976.

37) The Temple Emanuel was the second synagogue of the Congregation Emanuel, Denver's oldest Jewish congregation. The building was designed by architect John J. Humphreys and completed in 1898. It is now used as an auditorium and events center.

Two of the grandest churches in Denver were built within four blocks of each other. The Cathedral of St. John in the Wilderness, at 14th and Washington streets was constructed for the Episcopal congregation. Designed in the English Gothic style by the New York architectural firm of Gordon, Tracy, and Swarthwout, the cathedral was begun in 1905 and dedicated in 1908. A transept and apse with a central tower at the crossing were originally planned for the church, but never completed. A parish house was added on the southeast corner of the block in 1927. An educational and music building was built in the late 1950s, which connected the cathedral with the parish house.

In 1912, the Cathedral of the Immaculate Conception was opened. Located at Colfax and Logan, it was designed by Leon Coquard of Detroit in the French Gothic style and featured two 210-foot towers. It was designated as a minor basilica in 1979, and in August 1993 had the honor to host Pope John Paul II for the World Youth Day celebration. For that occasion, a meditation and sculpture garden was build adjacent to the cathedral on East Colfax.

38) *The Cathedral of St. John in the Wilderness, commonly known as St. John's Cathedral, is the third Episcopal church of that name. The church traces its history to the first St. John's in the Wilderness, which was consecrated in 1862.*

39) *Completed in 1912, the Cathedral of the Immaculate Conception is a French Gothic style cathedral that can seat 1,500 people. The church and an adjacent prayer garden were renovated in 1993 for a visit by Pope John Paul II.*

Other churches constructed after the turn of the century included First Church of Christ, Scientist at 1401 Logan, built in 1906; St. Andrew's Episcopal Church at 20th and Glenarm in 1909; and the 1910 Church of the Holy Redeemer at 20th and Williams. In 1926, two notable Catholic churches were completed: St. Dominic's at 29th and Federal and St. Cajetan's at Ninth and Lawrence, now a part of the Auraria Higher Education Complex.

Along with churches, new school buildings were needed to keep pace with neighborhood growth. Between 1893 and 1930, 70 elementary, junior high, and high schools were constructed for a school enrollment that reached more than 44,000 by 1930.

Many of the schools were built as part of a major $12 million expansion program after 1922. Among these were a new East High School (1925), West High School (1925), and South High School (1926). North High School had been put into service in 1911. During this period, the school district invested not only money but also careful planning

40) The Schearith Israel Synagogue, which closed in 1957, has been preserved on the Auraria Higher Education Center campus as a gallery. It was originally built in 1877 as an Episcopal church. When it was sold to the Jewish congregation, the structure was modified somewhat to its present configuration.

and design. As part of the City Beautiful ideal, many schools were located adjacent to parks or parkways, and the city's leading architects were hired to design them. North High is an outstanding example of Beaux-Arts style, East High favors English Jacobean, and West High's design was influenced by the Collegiate Gothic style.

A good portion of the elementary and junior high schools received the same careful design attention. Morey Junior High, at East 14th and Clarkson, was designed with Renaissance influences by Fisher and Fisher architects in 1921. Lake Junior High School (1926) was sited overlooking Sloan's Lake and designed in the Tudor style by Burnham Hoyt.

41) East High School is located on a broad esplanade which leads from Colfax Avenue to one of the main entrances to City Park. Its large windows are typical of schools of the era.

42) North High School was built in 1911 to relieve the overcrowding when it shared a same building with elementary grades in the Ashland School on West 29th Avenue. Former Prime Minister of Israel Golda Meir attended North High from February 1913 to June 1914.

Libraries also were considered important to the fabric of the developing neighborhoods. In addition to the main library in Civic Center, the city fathers considered branch libraries essential and were able to begin building, thanks to a $160,000 grant from the Andrew Carnegie Foundation in 1912. Eleven branches were constructed between 1913 and 1929, and many are still in service today.

As with schools, planners felt that the libraries should be part of the parks and parkway system. Library designers realized this idea by siting the Woodbury branch library in Highland Park (1913), the Decker branch in Platte Park (1913), and the Smiley branch in Berkeley Park (1918). The branch libraries also were designed by well-known architects of the day. Many of those still being used have been carefully remodeled and expanded with a sensitivity to their original design elegance.

43) Lake Junior High School (now Lake Middle School) was built in 1926 on a hill overlooking Sloan's Lake with a panoramic view of the Rocky Mountains.

44) Named for a Denver pioneer and one of the founders of the public library, General Roger W. Woodbury, the Woodbury branch library was built in Highland Park in North Denver. The building was completed in 1913 and designed in the Florentine Renaissance style.

At the turn of the century, all of the houses, churches, schools, and libraries were connected with a network of mostly dirt roads and streets. That was to change during the first few decades of the 1900s with the coming of the automobile. The citizens of Denver saw their first automobile in 1899, and the first car was advertised for sale in 1900. Denver issued its first automobile permit in 1906.

The automobile quickly gained popularity. By 1910, 5,220 vehicles were registered, and by 1915, that number had grown to about 8,300. Ten years later, more than 65,000 cars and over 4,700 trucks had permits. By 1930, nearly 85,000 cars and trucks were clogging Denver streets. To accommodate the new motorized buggies, the city began spending more money. During Mayor Speer's term, many city streets were paved, new bridges were constructed over Cherry Creek and the Platte River, and the 20th Street Viaduct was built.

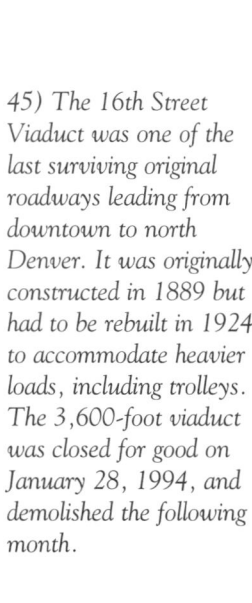

45) The 16th Street Viaduct was one of the last surviving original roadways leading from downtown to north Denver. It was originally constructed in 1889 but had to be rebuilt in 1924 to accommodate heavier loads, including trolleys. The 3,600-foot viaduct was closed for good on January 28, 1994, and demolished the following month.

In addition to enjoying the in-town convenience of the automobile, Denverites also began racing them on tracks like that in Overland Park, participating in cross-country contests, or simply taking a spin in the country or up the rough roads into the mountains.

Growth of other city services also continued to keep pace with the expanding neighborhoods. After the shakeout of all the private water companies late in the 19th century, the Denver Union Water Company, headed by Walter Cheesman and David Moffat, continued to slake the city's thirst until 1918. That year, Denver voters decided to purchase the company for $13.97 million, and it became the Denver Water Board. The purchase included the Capitol Hill pump station and reservoir, which had been completed in 1899, as well as Cheesman reservoir, which had been built in 1905.

46) *Walter Scott Cheesman started a drug store in Denver in 1860. He later built his empire with banking, railroads, real estate, and the water business. By 1894, he was president of the Denver Union Water Company. The present governor's mansion was originally built for Walter Cheesman, but he died before it was completed. (The Denver Public Library, Western History Department)*

47) This 1908 photograph shows the Capitol Hill pump station in Congress Park. The large reservoir is located under the planking at right. (Courtesy of Denver Water Department)

For gas and electricity, Denver citizens continued to rely on the Denver Gas and Electric Company, housed in the Gas and Electric Building that it had built at 15th and Champa in 1910. Denver Gas and Electric became Public Service Company of Colorado in June 1923, and by 1928 natural gas replaced coal gas.

48) A large Barr pump in the Capitol Hill pump station sucked water out of the reservoir and into city mains. (Courtesy of Denver Water Department)

During the city's expansion after the turn of the century, Denver's primary link with the rest of the country continued to be the railroad. That was to change around 1930 with the coming of the airplane.

Denverites saw their first flying machine on February 2, 1910, when Louis Paulhan assembled a biplane he had shipped to Denver in pieces and took off from the race track at Overland Park for a flight that only lasted a few minutes. Airplanes remained mostly a curiosity until after World War I, where they proved their practical worth.

The first commercial flight in Colorado was not until 1919, when Ira B. Humphreys formed the Curtiss-Humphreys Airplane Company. In 1922, Humphreys built a landing strip east of the city, a few blocks away from what was to become Stapleton airfield. He flew passengers to Colorado Springs, Wyoming, and Estes Park.

49) Airplane travel was a big event when the Denver Municipal Airport opened in 1929. Denver got its start into the air age for just $430,000, which bought the land, four gravel runways, a hanger, and a small terminal. (The Denver Public Library, Western History Department)

107

During the 1920s and 1930s, several fledgling airlines competed for what business there was, including the emerging airmail service. Among them was Colorado Airways, which started service in 1926, and linked Denver with the rest of the country's developing air transportation system. In 1927, Western Air Express offered airmail service between Denver and Pueblo. Later it provided mail and passenger service between Cheyenne, Denver, Colorado Springs, and Pueblo. Western Air Express later became Western Airlines.

To keep up with the growth of the airline industry and compete with airfields around the country, Mayor Benjamin Stapleton pushed for a city airport to replace the several makeshift airstrips that had developed since the introduction of the airplane. He proposed a site far east of the city near Sand Creek. Opponents to the plan called it "Stapleton's Folly," but Stapleton persisted and had the necessary land purchased for $143,000. To build four gravel runways and a small terminal and hangar, the city spent another $287,000 and dedicated Denver Municipal Airport on October 17, 1929. In 1930, lights were installed for night flights. It was renamed Stapleton Airfield in 1944 and, with many expansions and additions, served Denver for 65 years until Denver International Airport was opened.

The Ku Klux Klan in Colorado

Despite all of the positive growth occurring in the first three decades of the 20th century, Denver did not escape the ugly specter of prejudice and bigotry. Discrimination was especially prevalent against African-Americans, Jews, and Catholics. The underlying hatred reached its peak during the mid-1920s when the Ku Klux Klan, lead by John Galen Locke, held significant representation in Denver and Colorado politics.

The Klan's presence had spread to Colorado from the south in 1921. It started to exercise its political strength in 1923 by supporting the election of Mayor Benjamin Stapleton, who was a Klansman although he later publicly opposed the group. After Stapleton took office he appointed fellow Klansmen to many city jobs, including the chief of police.

In 1924, the Klan managed to get another member, Clarence Morley, elected as governor. They also established Colorado representation in the U.S. Senate with candidate Rice Means. Other Klan members were elected the same year as state legislators and as judges. Non-Klan members of the legislature managed to keep the organization in check, but during a two-year period the Klan made its presence obvious with march-

50) Ku Klux Klan rallies were common events around Denver in the early 1920s when many Klan members held political office. (The Denver Public Library, Western History Department)

es, cross burnings, open threats, and rallies on Table Mountain near Golden and Ruby Hill in west Denver.

The Colorado Ku Klux Klan began to fall apart in the early months of 1925 after a much-publicized kidnapping by some Klan members. That incident and continued resistance to the Klan by politicians and citizens alike, a federal charge of income tax evasion against Locke, and pressure from the Klan's national leadership eventually forced Lock to resign in July 1925.

Although Benjamin Stapleton had been a Klan member, owed his first election to the KKK, and initially supported some of its aims, he soon began to oppose them openly and started to clear the city administration of Klan members. With his dubious ties to the Klan severed, Stapleton began his long career as mayor. With the exception of a four-year period in the early 1930s, Stapleton oversaw the city's struggle with the great depression and its survival through World War II.

PART THREE

From Bad Times to Recovery, 1930 to 1945

On the day before Denver International Airport opened, thousands of workers began the largest moving project Denver had ever seen. Over an 18-hour period, everything from chairs to jetliners was moved 22 miles northeast to the new airport. Shortly after midnight on opening day, Denver's old Stapleton International Airport was officially decommissioned, the white stripes on its runways unceremoniously painted out, and large "X"s painted across the runways. The move marked the end of the airport that carried the name of one of Denver's most notable mayors: Benjamin F. Stapleton.

Like Mayor Stapleton, the promoters of Denver International were accused of building an airport too far from the city. But also like Stapleton, they knew that the city's growth, as well as that of the national airline system, demanded a location away from the sprawling metropolis.

When Benjamin Stapleton dedicated the Municipal Airport on October 17, 1929, it was the culmination of one of his goals as mayor: to connect Denver with the nation's expanding airline system so the city would not be bypassed as it was when the transcontinental railroad had been built.

Since his first-term election in 1923, Mayor Stapleton had been busy improving the city in other ways not as spectacular as the airport, but just as important. He began street-paving projects like Alameda Avenue, which was surfaced in 1926, and secured a franchise with Public Service Company to bring natural gas to the city in 1928. As the first major city in the country to get natural gas, Denver's air got noticeably cleaner as homes and businesses phased out coal heating.

1) Benjamin Stapleton was mayor of Denver for 20 years, from 1923 to 1931 and again from 1935 to 1947 As a conservative Democrat, he managed to remain popular by working with business as well as workers. (The Denver Public Library, Western History Department)

City and County Building Construction

One of the most significant building projects begun during Mayor Stapleton's tenure was the City and County Building. A city government building always had appeared on early plans for the Civic Center as a companion to the State Capitol on the east-west axis. Functionally, the municipal building was needed because the old City Hall at 14th and Larimer streets was obsolete and too small.

One of the most unique aspects of the City and County Building was the design process. When it was apparent that the city was serious about erecting a new city hall, the fraternity of Denver architects became interested. However, instead of fighting among themselves for the commission, the members of the Colorado Chapter of the American Institute of Architects (AIA) suggested that architectural services be handled by a coordinated effort of its members. To this end, the group formed the Allied Architects Association in July 1924. The Association consisted of all 39 Denver architects who were members of the AIA Colorado Chapter.

2) A group of 39 architects designed the City and County Building. Their proposed site plan showed a future building in the Civic Center to balance the existing library. (Courtesy of Ken Fuller)

Mayor Stapleton and the City Council signed a contract with the Association on December 3, 1924, for a fee of 6% of the construction cost. The architects intended that any profits from the fee be used to establish a trust fund for the purpose of advancing the interests of the profession in Colorado.

The Allied Architects Association developed two different designs for the building. One was a low, horizontal scheme defining a semicircular shape on the east side. The other design included a tower. After studying both approaches, the Association decided that a tower would be a detriment to the view from the State Capitol and not in keeping with the rest of the Civic Center. They formally adopted the low, horizontal design and presented it to the mayor and City Council in June 1925. The estimated cost was $4.5 million.

The mayor and council approved the design, but as soon as it was made public the controversy started. The *Denver Post* campaigned against it and many citizens disliked it. One citizens group even hired architect J. B. Benedict to come up with another design. His approach was a large building with a 350-foot tower of ornate Gothic design. Both *The Denver Post* and the *Rocky Mountain News* endorsed the Benedict scheme, but Mayor Stapleton and the City Council would not acquiesce.

3) *The City and County Building was designed so it would not block the view of the mountains from the steps of the State Capitol. The clock tower provides a distinctive feature without being intrusive. Kate Speer, widow of the former mayor, donated money for the tower clock and the carillon, which still rings the Westminster chimes every hour.*

Problems with bidding and a controversy over the use of Colorado stone or Indiana limestone delayed the project for several years. Even though all the money required was not available, ground was broken on March 26, 1929. As the project neared completion, another bond issue was approved by the voters to provide the necessary funds to complete the building.

When the building was dedicated on August 1, 1932, visitors saw a building in the modified Roman style 435 feet long and 273 feet wide using Colorado Cotopaxi granite for the lower portion and limestone for the upper stories.

The interior of the $4.7 million structure was finished in a variety of fine stones. Colorado travertine was used for the walls of the main corridor as well as the 19-foot-high columns in the main lobby, which are the tallest monoliths of travertine in the world. Colorado yule marble was used for the counters of the public offices and in the rest rooms, pink Tennessee marble for the floor borders and stair treads, Travernelle-Clair stone from Italy as courtroom trimming, and Roseal Tennessee marble for the main entrances to the offices. Other marble from Vermont and Italy was used in other parts of the building.

4) Corinthian columns dominate the pediment over the entrance to the City and County Building. The 26-foot-by-13-foot bronze doors originally cast for the entrance were the largest in the world at the time.

In addition to guiding the completion of the City and County Building, Stapleton also formed the Denver Planning Commission in 1926. When it issued its first report in 1929, the commission recommended widening streets, designing boulevards to connect an even larger park system than Mayor Speer had started, and constructing recreational centers. Before Stapleton could get a good start on these projects, a national crisis intervened. Barely more than a week after the new Municipal Airport was dedicated, the stock market crashed on October 29, 1929, marking the beginning of the great depression.

5) This photograph shows the City and County Building as it was nearing completion in 1932. The building with the small dome in the middle right of the picture is the Arapahoe County Courthouse. Some of the taller buildings included the telephone building in the top left of the picture and the Republic Building at the right of the courthouse. (The Denver Public Library, Western History Department)

115

Surviving the Depression

When the first planes flew onto the tarmac at the new airport in 1929, Denver and Colorado were enjoying relatively good times. Denver was the center of a growing regional market for manufacturing and wholesale and retail trade. The high prices during World War I had raised metals prices and encouraged farmers to convert dry lands into plowed fields to increase output. The city had one-fourth of the state's population and accounted for one-third of the value of products for the entire eastern Rocky Mountain region.

Except for the people who had extensive investments, the stock market crash had little immediate effect on Denver and Colorado. People were still optimistic into 1930, but by the end of the year businesses started laying off employees. The trend worsened in 1932 as agricultural and metals prices fell and more layoffs occurred. Businesses and banks began to fail. Trade and industry faltered. By 1933, unemployment was at 25%. Between 1929 and 1933, per capita income dropped 40% in Colorado.

The beginning of the drought on the eastern plains aggravated the problems. Southeastern Colorado was part of the dust bowl from 1933 to 1937. On average, the plains got six inches less precipitation per year than was required to raise crops. In 1934 alone, half of the crops in Colorado failed.

6) *As the depression closed in on Denver, people could still enjoy the free exhibits of the Denver Art Museum when some of its collection was housed on the fourth floor of the newly completed City and County Building. (Courtesy of Denver Art Museum)*

As Denverites began to feel the personal effects of the depression, the city and state governments did little. Neither the mayor nor the governor wanted to raise taxes to provide public assistance and instead simply cut expenses. One exception was governor William Adams' attempt to help the economy by expanding highway construction, thinking this would provide jobs. Some modest municipal help came in 1931, when many cities throughout the state encouraged people to grow their own subsistence gardens by giving them land, seed, equipment, and training. In Denver, newly elected mayor George Begole, who barely beat Stapleton in the 1931 election, created the Citizens' Unemployment Committee, but it was just to aid local charities. The Committee helped the Community Chest raise money, operated bread and milk kitchens, distributed discarded clothing, and attempted to find work for the unemployed.

In the early 1930s, people had to find other ways to survive. The Community Chest was some help as it spent about $1 million annually from the beginning of the depression until 1932 when contributions declined. Locally, the K & B Packing Company extended what help it could by giving away 10-pound bags of meat to the needy every Christmas. Some desperate people even tried panning for gold in the South Platte River in 1932. A few lucky souls found some flakes, but the idea turned out to be a fool's dream.

7) Early in the depression years, desperate citizens tried finding gold in the South Platte River as the pioneers had done. They had as little success, too. These men are taking a PWA class in gold panning. (The Denver Public Library, Western History Department)

In 1931 and 1932, most people turned to one of the dozens of self-help organizations for survival. At Grace Methodist Church the Reverend Edgar M. Wahlberg organized the Grace Self-Help Co-operative in 1931. It collected and dispensed food, gave free haircuts, and supplied firewood. Its members worked for farmers in exchange for a portion of the crops. They also picked up stale bread at bakeries for distribution and offered free repair services. Some of the well-to-do, like banker John Evans, donated money to help.

Another cooperative group was Denver's Unemployed Citizens' League, which started in June 1932. Members received credit for hours worked and got supplies according to the time they put in. Members picked ripening fruits and vegetables at nearby farms that farmers could not afford to harvest. They also salvaged edible, but not salable, food from merchants. They repaired abandoned homes to provide shelter for people who had been evicted, and provided clothing and transportation to other members. There were about 30,000 members working in 22 districts by the end of 1932.

As 1932 ended, private charity groups were running out of money and the depression was worsening. Conservative estimates placed the number of unemployed in Colorado at about 65,000, one-sixth of the state's workforce. The federal government began to provide assistance in January 1932 when Congress approved Herbert Hoover's Reconstruction Finance Corporation (RFC), which was initially designed to loan money to corporations, railroads, and banks. In July, the program was extended with the Emergency Relief and Construction Act, which extended RFC loans to the states. The states, in turn, were to use the money for direct giveaways to the destitute and for public works projects that would repay the loans. Late that year, Mayor Begole formed the Denver Emergency Relief Committee to distribute RFC money.

8) Petertown was a makeshift community around the South Platte River bottom near where McNichols Arena is today. This 1938 photo shows how desperate conditions were at that time. Petertown was founded by Peter "The Prophet" Therkelsen as a haven for aging men and a place for his religious cult. (Courtesy, Colorado Historical Society)

The New Deal for Denver

Real federal help did not come until 1933, when newly elected president Franklin D. Roosevelt started his New Deal Programs. From March 9 to June 16, 1933, Congress passed legislation creating an alphabet soup of assistance agencies, including the Federal Emergency Relief Administration (FERA), the Civil Works Administration (CWA), the National Recovery Administration (NRA), the Civilian Conservation Corps (CCC), the Agricultural Adjustment Administration (AAA), and the Public Works Administration (PWA).

Some of the early New Deal programs, like FERA, were direct money grants that required the states to provide matching funds. At first, Colorado politicians, including governor Ed Johnson, balked at the idea of handouts and federal assistance. The state legislature only authorized an insignificant $60,000 for all of 1933. The local administrator of FERA threatened to withhold any more federal money until Colorado did its share. Faced with rebellion by the unemployed, the legislature finally relented and voted in January 1934 to provide $2 million for relief, to which FERA added another $.5 million.

9) One of the make-work projects of the Civil Works Administration was placing riprap along the banks of the Platte River. In this 1934 photo, crews are finishing up a portion near 19th Street. (Courtesy of Colorado State Archives)

Through 1934, the FERA gave direct grants to individuals, donated to self-help cooperatives, established camps for transients, distributed surplus food, and created jobs for the unemployed. The Civil Works Administration (CWA) was part of FERA. In Denver, the CWA hired unemployed workers to perform jobs like placing riprap on the banks of Cherry Creek and the South Platte for flood control and making mattresses for the Denver Board of Public Welfare. The Colorado Historical Society benefited as a few people were hired to interview pioneers and some unemployed architects were enlisted to build a model of Denver as it was in the early 1860s.

By the end of the year, FERA was providing help to about one-fourth of Colorado's population. By the time FERA closed in late 1935, nearly $40 million had been spent by the agency in Colorado.

Another early New Deal program was the National Recovery Act, which attempted to fix prices, wages, and labor costs for a multitude of products and services. The program was short-lived because the U.S. Supreme Court declared it unconstitutional in 1935. FERA also was closed in 1935 as President Roosevelt began to realize that direct handouts were not the answer to the nation's problems. Programs that provided work for people, like the Civilian Conservation Corps (CCC), seemed to be a better approach.

The CCC had been authorized by Congress in March 1933, and was designed to train young men between the ages of 18 and 25 to work conserving farms, forests, parks, and protecting grazing lands. Its Colorado headquarters was at Fort Logan, and by 1938 CCC workers had planted more than 9 million trees, built about 87,000 check dams, and stocked waterways around the state with fish.

10) One of Denver's most popular legacies of the depression work programs is Red Rocks amphitheater, which seats more than 10,000. It is built between two huge stone outcroppings and has another building-size rock behind the stage. Civilian Conservation Corps (CCC) labor helped build much of the park.

One of the most notable CCC Denver projects was Red Rocks Amphitheater west of the city. The land for Red Rocks Park had been acquired by the city in 1928, but remained largely undeveloped during the early days of the depression. When Benjamin Stapleton was reelected in 1934 after the single term of George Begole, he appointed George E. Cranmer as Manager of Parks and Improvements. Cranmer had seen an ancient amphitheater in Sicily during his overseas travels and wanted to create one for Denver between two huge rock outcroppings in the park. Mayor Stapleton did not want to spend city money to develop the site. However, Cranmer managed to enlist the National Parks and Monuments Service of the CCC to build the theater, roads, parking lots, and walkways using only a modest amount of city funds. Working from a design by Denver architect Burnham Hoyt, construction began in 1935.

Another early make-work program of the New Deal that had a lasting effect on Denver was the Public Works Administration (PWA). The PWA was designed to provide money for large projects designed and man-

11) George Cranmer, who was named Manager of Parks and Improvements by Mayor Benjamin Stapleton in 1935, was instrumental in completing many of Denver's significant projects such as Red Rocks, the Valley Highway, and Stapleton Airport. Cranmer Park, at First Avenue and Clermont, is named in his honor. (The Denver Public Library, Western History Department)

aged by professionals, but which provided employment and needed facilities for cities and states. Denver's first request for PWA money was to divert Western Slope water from the Fraser River through the pioneer bore of the Moffat Tunnel. By 1936, the first water was flowing under the Continental Divide, and by 1938, the project was finished.

In Denver, PWA money helped build more than 12 miles of sewers, water treatment plants, and the Capitol Annex Building at 14th and Sherman. PWA gave $157,000 for the Boettcher School for Crippled Children at East 19th and Downing after Claude Boettcher donated $192,500. When Lawrence C. Phipps gave $137,500 of his money, the federal agency also granted $112,500 to build Phipps Auditorium at the Colorado Museum of Natural History. Another PWA grant helped construct the new police building at 1245 Champa in 1940. By the time the agency closed, it had granted money to 205 projects in Colorado at a total cost of $47.9 million.

12) When the State Office building became overcrowded, the legislature authorized the construction of the Capitol Annex Building that used PWA funds. The building was completed in 1939 and represented the emerging architectural design trends of the period. The low structure at left is the heating plant.

13) The old Police Building at 1245 Champa was a fine example of the International Style of architecture popular during and after the depression. It was completed in 1941, and a two-story addition was added later. It now is used for offices for the Denver Center for the Performing Arts.

Building on the idea that work programs were the best way to beat the depression, Congress authorized the Works Progress Administration (WPA) in April 1935. Unlike the PWA, the WPA was a make-work program for small and medium-sized projects. The list of Denver WPA work is long. WPA projects included improvements to Sloan's Lake, adding nine holes to the Berkeley Golf Course (now Case Municipal Golf Course), expanding the Overland Park golf course, constructing the Curtis Park swimming pool, and developing Bonnie Brae Park.

14) Stone was a popular building material for depression-era make-work projects. This boathouse at Sloan's Lake was a Works Progress Administration project and is still used.

Denver's unemployed also built the monkey island at City Park zoo, improved the Cherry Creek embankment between University and Colorado boulevards, and widened Grant, Logan, and West and East Colfax, among other streets. Additional construction projects included Hale Parkway between Colorado Boulevard and Grape Street and the extension of runways at the airport. WPA money was even used in 1937 to start converting the Agnes Phipps Memorial Sanatorium into a technical school for the Army Air Corps at Lowry Field as the first rumblings of war were being heard from Europe.

WPA projects did not stop with construction. As part of the Public Works of Art Project, unemployed Colorado artists were hired to beautify new and existing buildings. Sculptor Gladys Caldwell created a frieze for the City and County Building. Frank E. Mechau painted a mural titled "Horses at Night" for the Denver Public Library. Ethel Magafan embellished the South Denver Branch Post Office with her painting of "The Horse Corral."

The WPA had similar projects for writers, musicians, and actors suffering through the depression. One of the most notable products of the Federal Writer's Project was the publication in 1941 of *Colorado: A Guide to the Highest State.* The Federal Music Project in Denver gave musicians

15) This 1934 photograph shows workers in the sewing and tufting room of a mattress factory. The project was one of the many developed by the short-lived Federal Emergency Relief Administration to help the unemployed during the early days of the depression. (Courtesy of Colorado State Archives)

work from 1935 to 1940. It included three orchestras, a symphonic band, a string quartet, and various other orchestral and vocal performing groups. The Federal Theater Project hired a few actors to perform in the Baker Theater at 1447 Lawrence Street from 1936 until 1939. In addition to providing work, the plays and concerts presumably offered a diversion to everyone coping with hard times.

Although many people objected to the Works Progress Administration, as well as the other New Deal programs, the effect of the WPA on Denver and Colorado was dramatic. When it closed in 1943, more than 150,000 state residents had been employed on approximately 5,000 projects worth about $100 million. Four hundred structures had been built, including roads, dams, schools, recreation centers, offices, sewage disposal plants, and airports. Smaller projects included the indexing of several decades of the *Rocky Mountain News* for the Denver Public Library, sewing, book mending, and the operation of nursery schools. In Denver alone, Mayor Benjamin Stapleton estimated the value of WPA projects to the city to be about $50 million.

Times were hard during the depression, but life in the city went on. Denverites enjoyed radio, went to the movies for 25 cents or less, played the new game of Monopoly, and participated in the dance marathon

16) *The Works Progress Administration gave employment to artists as well as other workers. Here, two women chisel bas-reliefs on a slab in the hallway of the City and County Building when the Denver Art Museum was located there. (Courtesy of Colorado State Archives)*

craze. They watched amateur and semi-pro baseball and softball games as well as basketball and football. The University of Colorado and Denver University football teams were especially popular.

For stage entertainment, people went to the Central City Opera, which was reopened in 1932 after 50 years of inactivity. The Denver Symphony Orchestra was organized and performed its first concert on November 30, 1934. It was the descendant of three earlier orchestras, the original Denver Symphony, which played as early as 1900, the Denver Philharmonic Orchestra founded in 1919, and the Denver Civic Symphony which replaced the Philharmonic in 1922.

Prohibition was repealed in 1933, so those who could afford to drink did so. Denver's Tivoli Union Brewery and Golden's Coors brewery began shipping beer on April 7, 1933.

One of Denver's most distinctive contributions to popular culture during the depression was being the home of the invention of the cheeseburger. On March 5, 1935, Louis E. Ballast, the author's father, made an Application and Affidavit for Registration of Trade-Mark to the Colorado Secretary of State for the name "Cheeseburger," which he proposed to be used as the name of a sandwich. Ballast had developed the cheeseburger earlier at his restaurant, the Humpty Dumpty Barrel Drive-In, while experimenting with different toppings that could be placed on an ordinary hamburger.

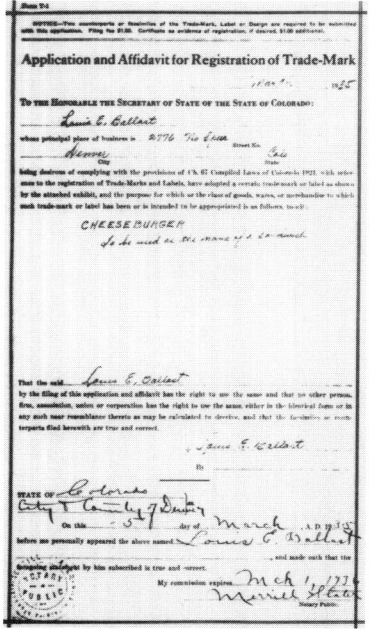

17) The cheeseburger was invented in Denver during the depression. This trademark application shows that the cheeseburger was invented by Louis Ballast, and a trademark application for use of the word was applied for on March 5, 1935. (Author's collection)

18) The first drive-in restaurant in Denver was born during the depression. In 1930, the original Humpty Dumpty Drive-In was a large barrel-shaped structure with flaps that were raised up for service. (Author's collection)

Ballast started his business in north Denver in 1930 in a small building that was shaped like a barrel. Originally there was no inside seating, but large flaps opened up so "car hops" could serve people in their cars. It was one of Colorado's first drive-in restaurants. An addition in 1933 provided some inside seating, and a completely new building was constructed in 1948. Ballast continued the drive-in restaurant until the early 1970s, making it a Denver institution for more than 40 years.

19) This is the building where the cheeseburger was invented early in 1935 at 2776 North Speer Boulevard. In 1933, Louis Ballast augmented the simple barrel-shaped building and added four booths and six stools for inside seating as well as drive-in service. It was replaced in 1948 with a new building at the same location. The waitresses always wore uniforms and had to look sharp! (Author's collection)

While Denverites munched on cheeseburgers, they could dream of skiing on the newly groomed slopes of Colorado's first ski areas made more accessible by new and improved roads. In the late 1930s, a small ski area was developed at the top of Berthoud Pass which included a rope tow. In 1937 George Cranmer, Manager of Parks and Improvements, began working on a plan to develop a ski area at the western portal of the Moffat Tunnel. Using some city money and Progress Works Administration money and labor, Cranmer oversaw what eventually would become Winter Park Ski area on land leased from the U.S. Forest Service. As an alternative to driving, Denverites could take a train through the Moffat Tunnel to the area. The special ski train made its first run on January 9, 1938, and has been serving those slopes ever since.

Denver During World War II

Skiing and other diversions of the depression did not last long. As New Deal money helped develop Lowry Field in the late 1930s, the war in Europe came closer to Denver. On December 7, 1941, the Japanese attack on Pearl Harbor pulled the country into World War II. In a short time, the war prompted the recovery from the depression, and Denver entered a new era of development.

20) Lowry Field in 1938 consisted primarily of the former Agnes Phipps Sanitorium, a clinic for tuberculosis patients. The first new additions were four temporary National Guard hangars. The intersection in the foreground is Sixth Avenue and Quebec Street. (Courtesy of Wings Over the Rockies Aviation and Space Museum)

Nearly all of the development of Denver during the first half of the decade was war-related. Lowry Field was dedicated in 1938 and was later renamed Lowry Air Force Base when the Air Force became an independent service in 1947. By 1944, Lowry had expanded to more than 600 buildings.

In 1941, the Remington Arms Company opened the Denver Ordnance Plant west of Denver at Sixth Avenue and Kipling Street to supply artillery shells and other ordnance to the war department. The federal government spent $20 million for the construction of 120 buildings, $87 million for ammunition, and another $14.8 million for equipment and management. Later, construction costs were estimated to have pumped $52 million into the local economy. The plant originally employed about 20,000 workers and was turned into the Denver Federal Center in 1946.

The Rocky Mountain Arsenal was established in 1942 northeast of the city to make napalm and gas bombs. Its cost was estimated at $62 million, and it offered jobs to about 14,000 people. The immediate effect helped

21) After the Denver Ordnance Plant was converted to the Denver Federal Center in 1946, it became one of the largest concentrations of federal government employees in the metropolitan area. Today, it still houses many federal agencies and programs such as the National Ice Core Laboratory, which helps study how climate changes, global warming, and solar activity have occurred during the past 250,000 years. (Courtesy of General Services Administration)

the local economy, but as a result of years of spills and haphazard disposal during government nerve gas manufacturing and pesticide production, by 1988 the site had been called the most polluted place in America.

Elsewhere around Denver, Buckley Field was built in mid-1942, Camp George West training camp near Golden was enlarged, a medical supply depot was built at 38th and York streets, and Fitzsimons Army Hospital was enlarged. Fitzsimons originally had been built in 1918 during World War I, but a new hospital was built for the latest conflict for 3.5 million.

Even the airport saw action. Renamed Stapleton Airfield in 1944, it was enlarged and runways were lengthened to accommodate the army bombers and cargo planes. Construction on the Denver Modification Center at the airport began in 1942. The $5 million facility was used to equip planes for war service.

The war benefited Denver in many ways. In addition to all the large government construction projects, smaller Denver businesses prospered as they supplied everything from parachutes to food products. Employment was so high that there was actually a shortage of workers as men,

22) Fitzsimons Army Hospital in Aurora is one of the largest military medical installations in the country. First established in 1918, the base was subsequently enlarged to serve the wounded of World War II. It was named after Lt. William Thomas Fitzsimons, who was the first American officer to die in World War I.

and some women, went off to the war. Even after the war was over, the federal government presence in Denver was everywhere. One study showed that by June 1946, there were more than 16,400 federal employees in the metropolitan area.

Although the economy was strong, the war years were not without their hardships. Everyone had to ration certain critical commodities like gasoline, rubber, meat, shoes, sugar, and butter. The Office of Price Administration (OPA) controlled the allocation of many of these commodities and controlled prices of dozens of products to keep inflation under control. To help the war effort, Denverites salvaged and recycled things like iron, copper, aluminum, rubber, and even fat. Victory gardens sprouted and people put their extra money into War Bonds.

23) During the war, the Office of Price Administration tried to stem inflation by controlling prices. This 1943 list from a Denver restaurant shows hamburgers priced at 15 cents and coffee at a nickel. (Author's collection)

24) This is the main building of the Agnes Phipps Sanitorium, circa 1942, after it was converted to the headquarters for the Lowry Technical Training Center. It served as the Summer White House for President Dwight D. Eisenhower in the early '50s, but was razed in 1963. (Courtesy of Wings Over the Rockies Aviation and Space Museum)

As the war ended in 1945, Mayor Stapleton was finalizing one of his last significant actions by selling a piece of city real estate. When the City and County Building was completed in 1932, the old Arapahoe County courthouse at 16th and Tremont Place was abandoned and demolished. The site was turned into a city park waiting for development. In 1945, an offer of $750,000 was made by William Zeckendorf, executive vice president of the New York development firm Webb and Knapp, Inc. Another offer was made by a Denver syndicate for a slightly higher price, prompting a bidding war which eventually was won by Webb and Knapp for $818,600. It was to be the beginning of another boom cycle for Denver.

PART FOUR

Growth After World War II: 1945 to 1973

Readers of the *Denver Business Journal* today get their news from the descendant of one of Denver's most outspoken and incisive independent newspapers born in the aftermath of World War II: *Cervi's Rocky Mountain Journal.* Eugene Cervi started his publication as a newsletter on August 5, 1945, during the same month Japan surrendered and officially ended the war. Cervi had been a reporter for both the *Rocky Mountain News* and the *Denver Post*, but was angered by what he felt were the isolationist attitudes of both daily papers during the war. He started *Cervi's Newsletter* to inform Denver businessmen and newcomers about the trends and events that he saw affecting the city and Colorado as America converted to a civilian economy.

When Eugene Cervi started his newsletter, Colorado's economy still was based on mining, ranching, and agriculture. There were few new industries. Most existing businesses had recovered from the depression thanks to the war, but the economy was stagnant. The civic and business leaders of Denver were descendants of the ruling families of earlier days.

1) Eugene Cervi published Cervi's Newsletter *and later* Cervi's Rocky Mountain Journal *from 1945 until 1970. Cervi provided an alternative and often lively view of events and people changing Denver and the Rocky Mountain region after the war as the metropolitan area began another era of growth. (The Denver Public Library, Western History Department)*

The developed area of the city only extended to Regis College on the north, Denver University on the south, Lowry Air Force Base on the east, and Sloan's Lake on the west. However, Denver was poised for growth.

The Post-World War II Boom

As with the rest of the country, war's end was a huge catalyst for change in Denver. A large number of the military and civilian people that had either worked in the city or passed through it during the conflict decided to make Denver or one of the surrounding counties their home. With the influx of newcomers and the beginning of the "baby boom" years, the population grew rapidly. By 1950, 563,832 people made Denver, Adams, Arapahoe, and Jefferson counties their home. Another 48,296 people lived in Boulder County.

Denver's post-war growth also was sparked by the conversion of many war-related industries around the city into peacetime federal government installations. The new technologies that had been developed during the war by local industries also were ripe for further development and use in the post-war economy.

2) *Denver in 1948 had changed little in 20 years. The Daniels and Fisher tower was still one of the tallest buildings in town, and there was still plenty of open space between the city and the foothills. (Courtesy of Wings Over the Rockies Aviation and Space Museum)*

However, before any significant expansion could happen, the political and economic structure of Denver had to change. At the end of the war, city government maintained a cozy relationship with the big names in business and banking. The power structure was a closely knit organization of private interests and an aging government headed by Mayor Stapleton, who was 75 in 1945.

Gene Cervi publicized the need to replace the old guard. In his newsletter of August 6, 1945, Cervi sarcastically listed the ages of the "dynamic builders of the Rocky Mountain region" including Charles Boettcher I, 93; banker Gerald Hughes, 70; ex-U.S. Senator Lawrence C. Phipps, Sr., 83; William C. Shepherd, editor and publisher of the *Denver Post*, 71; and Charles C. Gates, 68.

3) The Boettcher family was one of Denver's most wealthy and influential families. Charles Boettcher I (center) made much of his fortune in mining investments, and started the Great Western Sugar Company, the Ideal Cement Company, and a brokerage firm. His son, Claude K. Boettcher (left), continued the empire. Claude's son, Charles Boettcher II, is on the right. (The Denver Public Library, Western History Department)

Change began in 1946 when Palmer Hoyt was hired by the *Denver Post* to become its new editor and publisher. Until that time, the *Post* had been a profitable but sensationalistic newspaper from the time it was founded by Frederick Bonfils and Harry Tammen in 1895. After Bonfils died in 1933, the newspaper was taken over by his daughter, Helen, who hired William Shepherd as editor in 1933. Shepherd continued the *Post* tradition of sensationalism and reader-pleasing content until 1946, when Hoyt was charged with the responsibility to make the *Denver Post* a more respectable newspaper.

With the mayoral election coming up, Palmer Hoyt recognized the opportunity to replace Mayor Stapleton with someone who could bring about the changes he felt the city needed. Although he had served Denver well, Stapleton was unprepared for the post-war boom. At a breakfast meeting in Denver honoring U.S. Supreme Court Justice William O. Douglas, Hoyt was introduced to a 35-year old law school graduate, James Quigg Newton, who had been Douglas' law clerk before World War II. In Newton, Hoyt saw a perfect candidate for mayor.

With the backing of the *Denver Post*, the *Rocky Mountain News*, and both Republicans and Democrats alike, J. Quigg Newton was easily elected in 1947. Even Gene Cervi helped in the campaign.

As most everyone hoped, Newton did make significant changes to city government. Among other accomplishments, he updated the operation of many of the ordinary city services like trash collection, sewage disposal, and the coroner's office. Property taxes were assessed more equitably and city contracts for services and purchases were sent out for open, competitive bidding. An amendment to the city charter in 1954 created the Career Service Authority, which removed city employees, except for mayoral cabinet heads and a few city positions, from political appointment. Instead, they were hired and fired based on merit.

To help guide the city's growth in the post-war years, Newton replaced the Denver Planning Commission in 1949 with the Denver Planning Office, headed and staffed by professional planners and directed by a

4) At the Summer White House at Lowry Air Force Base in 1953, President Dwight D. Eisenhower discussed the post-armistice situation in Korea with (left to right) Assistant Secretary of State for Far Eastern Affairs Walter S. Robertson, United Nations Ambassador Henry Cabot Lodge, and Secretary of State John Foster Dulles. (Courtesy of Wings Over the Rockies Aviation and Space Museum)

nine-member board. In 1952, Mayor Newton helped get the 1908, 12-story building height limitation repealed. Until 1952, the Daniels and Fisher tower was the tallest building in town.

While the repeal of the height restriction encouraged bricks-and-mortar development in the early 1950s, the continuing presence of the federal government fueled the population growth and offered increasing employment opportunities. After World War II, the Denver Ordnance Plant was converted into the Denver Federal Center for a variety of federal agencies. Lowry Air Force Base continued to be used as a training center until September 30, 1994, when it was closed as part of the overall cutback in military installations around the country. Buckley Air National Guard Base remained as the home for the Colorado Air National Guard. Fitzsimons Army Hospital, located in Aurora, still serves as a major army medical facility. Northeast of the city, the Rocky Mountain Arsenal stayed open, manufacturing chemical pesticides and storing the chemical weapons produced during the war.

5) Lowry Air Force Base in 1958 was still an active military installation and major training facility for rocket, missile, and nuclear weapon systems. Fairmont cemetery is on the right, and the intersection of East Sixth Avenue and Quebec Street is near the lower left. (Courtesy of Wings Over the Rockies Aviation and Space Museum)

In 1953, Rocky Flats was built between Denver and Boulder as a top-secret plant to make plutonium triggers for nuclear weapons. At the time, it was welcomed as another boost to the local economy, but recent fires, disposal problems, and leakages have forced the plant to cease production and start a massive cleanup effort. Elsewhere, the Air Force Finance Center and the Air Reserve Records Center employed even more people, who made Denver their home in the early 1950s.

The effect of the federal government presence was significant. By 1959, it was estimated that there were about 20,000 civilian government employees in the Denver metropolitan area earning about $85 million per year, and another 11,000 people on the military payroll.

With more people, a large federal government presence, the large economic base of the existing industries, and a new city administration, Denver was on the brink of yet another surge in growth as the decade of 1940 neared its end. Eugene Cervi sensed this and knew the coming years would be important for the city. He changed his newsletter to a weekly newspaper and renamed it on September 22, 1949.

Still filled with business news and Cervi's opinions and observations, *Cervi's Rocky Mountain Journal*, as he stated in the September 22, 1949, issue, was directed "to readers bent on full and spirited living in these Continental Divide States. . . . Emphasis will be on commercial items because ours is a civilization in which America is destined by events to a culture of commerce.' Maintaining his position as journalistic gadfly until his death, Cervi wrote about what he saw as the needs of the city and the state, and was never afraid to question, prod, and expose the actions of business and political leaders.

Denver's New Building Boom

Some of the many prophetic ideas Gene Cervi had for Denver when he started his publication included a new art museum, a convention center, a baseball park, a football stadium, new theaters, museums, and a zoo along with superhighways to the suburbs. Some of these ideas were realized in the 1950s, 1960s, and 1970s, while others, like the baseball stadium, only recently have come to fruition.

The first surge of privately financed growth after the war came from out-of-state developers. William Zeckendorf, executive vice president of New York's Webb and Knapp, Inc., came to Denver in 1945 to purchase the site of the old Arapahoe County courthouse at 16th and Tremont Place. Webb

6) *Bears Stadium opened in August 1948 for the Denver Bears baseball team. Built on the site of an old garbage dump, the original 20,000-seat stadium has been enlarged several times to 76,000 seats to accommodate the Denver Broncos football team. It is now called Mile High Stadium. (The Denver Public Library, Western History Department; Photo by O. Roach)*

and Knapp eventually got title to the property in 1948 after a lengthy legal battle. It also purchased most of the block across Court Place.

After several years of planning and arranging for financing, construction on the Courthouse Square Project began in 1955 for what became the Hilton Hotel and the new home for the May D & F Department Store. The complex was designed by architect I. M. Pei, and when it was completed in 1958, it included an underground garage with parking for 1,500 cars and a bridge over Court Place connecting the hotel with the store. The department store block included what was then considered an ultra-modern hyperbolic paraboloid structure separate from, but connected to, the main store and a depressed skating rink. Shortly after Foley's bought the May D & F stores, it closed the downtown store in 1993. By mid-1994 the building remained vacant, awaiting either redevelopment or demolition.

About the same time Zeckendorf was working on the Courthouse Square Project, he became involved in the U. S. National Bank Building project at 17th and Broadway. Boettcher Associates was planning the bank building, but Zeckendorf originally had worked out a partnership agreement with them for a 50% interest in his project for a like share in the bank project. The agreement eventually was canceled in 1953, and Zeckendorf completed both projects.

7) Out-of-state developers discovered post-war Denver as a good place to make money. William Zeckendorf and Webb and Knapp, Inc., bought the old courthouse square property and developed the May D & F Department Store and the Hilton Hotel in the mid-1950s. (The Denver Public Library, Western History Department)

Like the Courthouse Square Project, the Mile High Center, as it became known, was designed by I. M. Pei. It included a 23-story office tower, a separate building for banking operations, a third structure under a spacious vaulted roof, and an open courtyard. The complex, completed in 1955, was masterfully designed and, like Courthouse Square, showed Denver a type of business development and architecture and urban planning it had never seen before. In the September 14, 1950, edition of *Cervi's Journal*, Gene Cervi said of the New York developer: "William Zeckendorf jarred the vegetating real estate brains of the community . . . tutored them on property values."

8) The Mile-High Center was Denver's first premier example of urban architecture and planning. Designed by architect I. M. Pei, the complex featured a courtyard and pond, and was home for the Denver U. S. National Bank. The complex was extensively remodeled in the mid-1980s, when the open plaza areas were enclosed by a glass-topped atrium. (The Denver Public Library, Western History Department)

Two other buildings that changed the look of downtown in the 1950s were also built by out-of-state developers. Two Dallas oil millionaires, Clinton and John Murchinson, bought the old Denver Club at 17th and Glenarm in 1953. Originally opened in 1888, the elegant sandstone building had housed the club first founded by David Moffat, Walter Cheesman, Henry Wolcott, and other movers and shakers of early Denver. The Murchinsons had the building razed and built a new 23-story, $6.5 million office building in 1954 that included the club on the top floors.

After the success of their first Denver project, the brothers started planning for another office tower across the street at 17th and Welton. During the planning and construction phases, the First National Bank decided to move into the structure, and by the time it was opened, it was named the First National Bank Building. The 28-story structure was completed in 1958 and included a gift shop and observation platform on the southwest half of the roof. The other half of the roof sported Denver's first heliport, although it was never used commercially as it had been designed. An additional floor was added to the rooftop area in the late 1960s for a penthouse suite of offices.

9) *The First National Bank Building was considered by many Denverites to be the city's first skyscraper when it was completed in 1958. At 28 stories with an observation deck on the roof, people could finally look down on the Daniels and Fisher Tower. (Courtesy of First Interstate Bank; Photo by Robert W. Schott)*

The new post-war development by out-of-state money illustrated the conservative practices of local banks. Most—like the First National Bank, the Colorado National Bank, and the Denver National Bank— kept their loan-to-deposit ratios low. Gene Cervi campaigned against what he felt were restrictive policies of the 17th Street banks, which were retarding the growth of housing and business in a critical time in Denver's history. In part because of Cervi's editorial prodding and in part because of competition and changing times, the city's banks eventually began to loosen their purse strings. Central Bank and Trust Company was one of the first when it started the revolutionary practice of concentrating on small business loans and consumer banking. In the 1950s, it remodeled its old building at 15th and Arapahoe streets and added a new drive-up facility to better serve the ever-increasing number of automobiles in the city.

On Capitol Hill, the skyline was also changing. The Sherman Plaza Apartment Building at Ninth and Sherman streets was constructed in 1952. At 17 stories, it proclaimed to be Denver's first tall building in 20 years, predating by a few years the new development just beginning in the central business district. Later in the decade, additional old houses and

10) *After the war, apartment buildings started getting larger, just like office buildings. The Sherman Plaza Apartment building was perched on Capitol Hill and still offers a spectacular view of the mountains.*

some of the early Denver mansions were being torn down to make way for apartments. In 1956 alone, 26 apartment buildings were built on Capitol Hill. In 1957, the 12-story Lanai Apartments at Eighth and Washington was opened. A year later the Versaille Apartments was completed at Eighth and Clarkson.

As the post-war population increased and Denver's economy boomed, additional development came fast. Some of the major downtown projects included the Petroleum Club Building, completed in 1959, the 655 Broadway Building, and the 22-story Brown Palace West Tower, which was opened in April 1959. In the next decade, the Western Federal Savings Building at 17th and California was completed in 1962, the 31-story Security Life Building with its penthouse restaurant in 1964, and the 42-story Brooks Towers apartments in 1967.

11) *Tall buildings continued to sprout up during the 1960s. The Security Life Building was completed in 1964 and included Denver's first glass-enclosed elevator, which took people to a top-floor restaurant. The restaurant is now closed, and the first two floors of the building have been substantially remodeled.*

On the outskirts of the city, new buildings were sprouting as fast as they were downtown. As with the office towers, much of the growth came from out-of-state industries wanting to move to Denver. The new businesses represented the beginning of Denver as a center for high-technology industries. Most of the newcomers were manufacturing concerns involved with the defense establishment, electronics, and aviation. The Baltimore-based Glenn L. Martin Company opened a plant in 1959 to manufacture rockets. In 1961, the name was changed to the Martin-Marietta Corporation. Ramo-Wooldridge Corporation of Los Angeles built southeast of the city and made guided missiles and computers. The Illinois-based Sunstrand Machine Tool Company opened Sunstrand Denver to assemble constant-speed alternating-current generators for jet aircraft.

Other high-tech pioneers included Ball Brothers Research Corporation, Stanley Aviation Corporation, Heckethorn Manufacturing and Supply Company, Hathaway Instrument, and the locally based C. A. Norgren Company. The first industrial park within a Colorado city also was built in the 1950s. It was the Littleton Industrial Park near 5400 South Delaware. As a model for industrial and business parks to come, the 30-acre development, completed in 1957, included a 50,000 square foot building for Norgren-Stemac, Inc., and a building for Metron Instrument Company set on spacious landscaped grounds with ample parking and a pond.

12) Since the early 1960s, the Martin Marietta company southwest of Denver has been one of Littleton's major employers, building Titan missiles for the country's space and defense programs. In June 1994, the company announced that it would move its Atlas rocket and Centaur rocket-booster design and assembly operations to Colorado from California. (Courtesy of Martin Marietta)

Established, local companies also grew after the war. By 1957, the Gates Rubber Company was the largest private employer in the metropolitan area with a payroll of 5,500. It was the sixth-largest rubber manufacturer in the country and is famous for its tires, industrial V-belts, and rubber hoses. At the time, there was a Gates retail outlet in every city of 5,000 or more in the United States. After cutting back Colorado operations, Gates employment in the state was about 1,500 in 1994.

Close to Gates on South Broadway was the Samsonite Division of Shwayder Brothers, a national leader in luggage manufacturing. Between 1946 and 1956, sales of Samsonite luggage had grown from $3 million to $50 million. At the time, one-fourth of the total volume of luggage business in the U.S. came from the Samsonite factory on South Broadway, which also manufactured school furniture, card tables, and mobile serving carts.

Farther west, in Golden, the Coors brewery had been expanding. In 1957, it employed 600 people in its brewery division, compared with 370 in 1946. By 1957, Coors was slaking the thirst of Colorado beer lovers by turning out more than a million barrels of beer a year. The Coors porcelain plant had 490 workers in 1957, compared to 230 just ten years earlier. By 1994, Coors employed about 5,000 people in Colorado.

13) *Purchased in 1911 by Charles Gates, the Colorado Tire and Leather Company expanded from a small firm making steel-studded leather tire covers into one of Denver's largest industrial plants. In 1919, it was renamed the Gates Rubber Company and moved to its present location at 999 South Broadway. (Courtesy of Gates Rubber Company)*

To meet the needs of the expanding population after World War II and to accommodate the privately funded growth in the city, public improvements struggled to keep pace. During Quigg Newton's administration in the early 1950s, additions were made to Stapleton Airport as well as the Museum of Natural History. The sewage disposal plant was expanded, and 2,300 public housing units were constructed. Downtown, an annex was constructed adjacent to Robert Speer's City Auditorium in 1952, which became the Auditorium Arena used for basketball and other sporting events. The City Auditorium was remodeled in 1956 as the Auditorium theater for stage productions and the Denver Symphony Orchestra. The Denver Coliseum was built next to the stock show grounds to accommodate the National Western Stock Show rodeo as well as other sporting events and large gatherings.

As always in Denver's history, water was vital to the growth of the metropolitan area. However, after the war, much of the growth was beyond the city limits, and the Denver Water Board recognized the difficulty in supplying water to thousands and thousands of new homes and businesses. During the terms of Mayors Stapleton and Newton, Denver had tried to get additional water supplies from the western slope.

Disputes in court between governments on the east and west sides of the Continental Divide over water rights held up any progress on new water supplies in the early 1950s. A severe drought in 1955 and 1956 forced the Water Board to institute water restrictions and draw a "blue

14) *The Denver Coliseum was completed in the early 1950s to provide more space for the overcrowded Stock Show Arena across the street. It is still used for National Western Stock Show and Rodeo events as well as other sports activities.*

line" beyond which it would not supply water to the suburbs until additional sources were found. As a result, more than 200 special water and sanitation districts were formed outside the blue line in the metropolitan area to serve the post-war growth.

When an agreement was finally reached between eastern and western slope interests, work began in earnest on the Blue River project, which included building Dillon Reservoir and the 23-mile long Harold D. Roberts Tunnel under the Continental Divide. The tunnel was completed in 1962, the reservoir began storing water in 1963, and water first flowed through the tunnel on October 27, 1964. The completion of the project doubled the water supply to Denver and the suburbs, and erased the blue line.

Additional water projects in the 1950s included improvements to the Vasquez canal system, a new Vasquez tunnel, enlargement of the Williams Fork Reservoir, and completion of Gross Reservoir in Boulder County.

15) An ever-increasing water supply continues to make Denver's growth possible. At the formal opening ceremony at the east portal on July 17, 1964, water flowed through the Harold D. Roberts tunnel from Dillon Reservoir into the North Fork of the South Platte River and then on to the Marston Filter Plant. The reservoir doubled the city's water supply. Mayor Thomas Currigan is the fifth person from the left. (Courtesy of Denver Water Department)

16) Denver gets its water from mountain snow melt delivered through a complex web of rivers, reservoirs, tunnels, and treatment plants. (Courtesy of Denver Water Department)

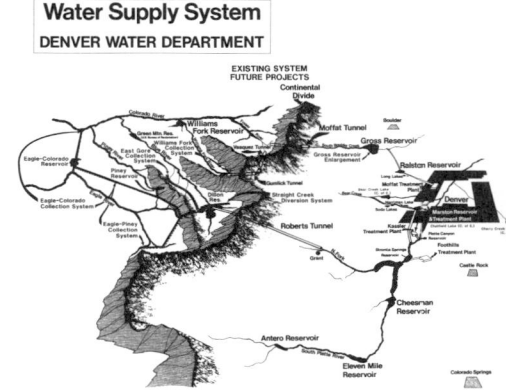

As Denver grew, regional planning became more important to the city as well as the surrounding suburbs. Mayor Newton's creation of the Denver Planning Office in 1949 was a start, but a broader view was needed. In April 1955, the Inter-County Regional Planning Commission was formed by a joint action of the commissioners of Adams, Arapahoe, and Jefferson counties and by the mayor and City Council of Denver. Douglas County joined the group in 1956. The Commission was created to make plans for the orderly growth of the metropolitan area covering nearly 3,800 square miles including 26 separate municipalities and more than 110 special districts. The Commission was the precursor of the Denver Regional Council of Governments (DRCOG), which was formed in 1958.

In addition to the positive growth occurring in the region, by the 1950s Denver also was showing signs of age. In the early part of the decade, city officials and civic leaders became concerned about the deterioration of some parts of downtown. In 1954, Downtown Denver Incorporated was created to organize the business community and formalize future action.

In 1955, a group from the Urban Land Institute studied the situation and recommended that Denver should undertake an urban renewal program for the lower downtown area. An Urban Renewal Division of the Department of Public Works was created in April 1955 as a means of dealing with slums and blighted areas that the city and many civic leaders thought constituted a growing menace. A few years later, in 1958, the Denver Urban Renewal Authority (DURA) was formed as a separate city agency.

17) In the late 1960s, the urban renewal mentality was to bulldoze the old to make way for the new. Downtown Denver lost many of its significant historic structures during the Skyline Urban Renewal Project, including the main portion of the Daniels and Fisher store, which was razed in February 1971. Prudential Plaza is rising in the background.

After starting a few projects in the Avondale district near Federal Boulevard and Colfax Avenue and in the lower downtown area, DURA began feasibility studies for revitalizing a large portion of downtown called the Skyline Urban Renewal Project. This was after a recommendation made in the Development Guide for Downtown Denver authored by the Downtown Denver Master Plan Committee in 1963. The voters rejected the idea in 1964, but approved it in the 1967 election. This was after an amendment to the U.S. Housing Act of 1965 allowed Denver to get a grant from the Department of Housing and Urban Development of $26 million (later raised to $33 million) for the project, based on allowing construction of the new $11.45 million Currigan Convention Hall to count as the city's contribution to the project.

In addition to approving money for Currigan Hall, Denver voters in 1964 also approved bond issues for a new $9 million Denver General Hospital building, $750,000 for a Juvenile Hall addition, $600,000 for street improvements, $1 million for parks and recreation improvements, and $2.3 million for flood control for Harvard Gulch.

18) *Currigan Convention Hall helped provide Denver's portion of funding for the Skyline Urban Renewal Project so the city could get federal money. The facility was soon deemed too small for many conventions, so the Colorado Convention Center was built across the street in 1990. This photograph was taken shortly after Currigan Hall opened. (Courtesy of Denver Convention Complex)*

A year later, Denver voters saw how important flood control could be. Late in the afternoon of June 16, 1965, after several days of heavy rains, thunderstorms south and west of Denver poured water into Plum Creek and Cherry Creek. The Cherry Creek dam, built in 1951, held back the rain flow along that waterway, but Plum Creek drained into the Platte River. Through the early evening hours, a wall of water and debris, picked up along the water's path, flowed through the central Platte Valley, causing havoc from Littleton to Denver until it dissipated north of town. The resulting flood caused an estimated $325 million in destruction and heavily damaged the lowlands west of the downtown area. The potential for future floods was minimized with construction of Chatfield Reservoir, but the disaster prompted more serious thinking about how the Platte Valley between downtown Denver and the river could be developed.

Growth continued in Denver through the 1960s, requiring even more public improvements. The voters once again responded in 1972 by approving bond issues for eight projects totaling more than $87.6 million. These included money for a new performing arts center, branch libraries, housing development, police and fire buildings, parks and recreation facilities, sanitary and storm sewers, a sports arena, and vehicle service facilities.

19) *The June 1965 flood of the Platte River destroyed much of the Platte Valley near downtown Denver. The flood was made worse when debris got caught under bridges and viaducts along the way. (The Denver Public Library, Western History Department; Photo by George E. Meister, Jr.)*

As Denver grew, public and private development as well as urban renewal began to threaten the city's heritage. Historic structures, dilapidated as they might have been, were being razed to make way for the new. By 1960, many of the early Denver mansions on Capitol Hill already had been torn down for new apartments, and most of Auraria, Denver's oldest neighborhood, would soon be demolished for the new Auraria Higher Education Complex. Lower downtown was also threatened as plans for the Skyline Project were finalized. It was in this climate that the historic preservation movement began.

One of the first efforts at saving part of Denver's past was taken when Dana Crawford and her husband John Crawford formed Larimer Square Associates in 1963 to preserve one block of Larimer Street between 14th and 15th streets. Its members included future Congresswoman Pat Schroeder. Ultimately, the buildings along this block of Larimer Street were restored and transformed into an exciting mix of shops, offices, galleries, restaurants, bars, and nightclubs. Even today, Larimer Square is a thriving area for residents and one of the most popular destination points for tourists along what General William Larimer once called "the best" street.

20) One block of buildings on Larimer Street between 14th and 15th streets escaped the bulldozers of the Skyline Urban Renewal Project by being developed into Larimer Square in the early 1960s. It was one of Denver's first major historic preservation projects.

In 1967, the Denver Landmark Preservation Commission was established. Its purpose was to designate buildings, structures, and neighborhoods that had historic value and to hold public hearings on whether to recommend landmark status to the City Council. If someone wants to demolish a building with landmark status for new development, there is a one-year hold placed on the demolition permit. This is designed to allow time for design review and negotiation with the developer to determine if the structure can be saved while still allowing economic use of the property.

A year after the Landmark Preservation Commission was formed, City Council passed the Mountain View Preservation ordinance to protect views of the mountains from Cheesman, City, and Ruby Hill parks as well as from the steps of the State Capitol by limiting heights of new buildings.

In 1970, a private organization, Historic Denver, was founded when the Molly Brown House was threatened with demolition. A year later, the organization bought the house for $80,000 and restored it as a museum. Today it is a popular destination point for both tourists and area residents. Since

21) *The Mountain View Preservation Ordinance protects the view of the Rocky Mountains from several places around Denver. Unfortunately, a few projects west of Cheesman Park slipped through before the ordinance took effect.*

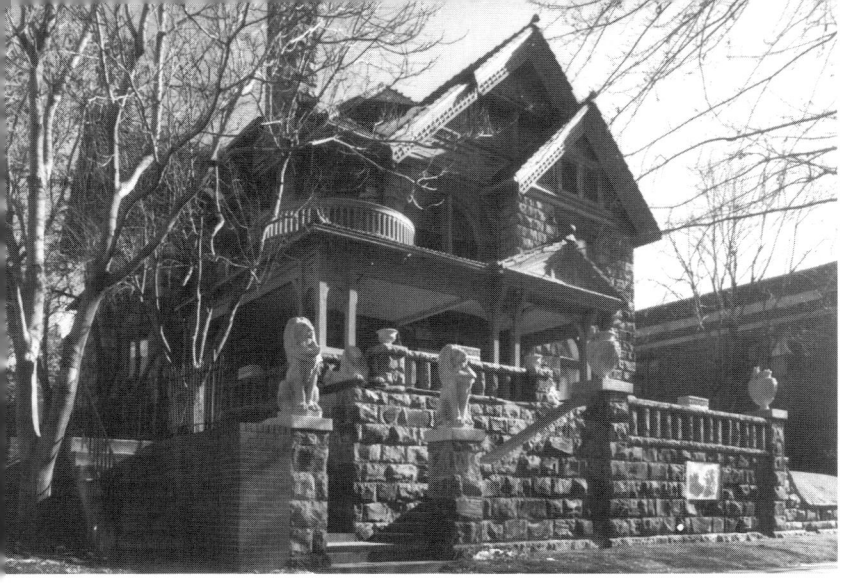

22) The House of Lions at 1340 Pennsylvania Street was the home of James J. Brown and his wife, Margaret, the "Unsinkable Molly Brown." The Browns made their fortune in mining in Leadville and moved to Denver in 1894. She became famous when she saved many people during the sinking of the Titanic.

that time, among other activities, Historic Denver has helped promote the restoration of the Curtis Park neighborhood, participated in taking inventory of Denver's historic buildings, helped restore a block of Victorian houses along Ninth Street on the Auraria Higher Education Center campus, and restored the Four Mile House, which it now operates as a museum.

23) The Four Mile House was originally a log inn established in 1859 as the last stop before Denver along the Smoky Hill Trail. It was later purchased and turned into a ranch and farm. Today, it is a museum at 614 South Forest Street.

Transportation Changes

Post-World War II growth required improved transportation, both locally with roads, highways, and bus service, and nationally with rail and airline service. Locally, the growth of the city and suburbs strained the capacity of the street system. When the war ended, there were no freeways or high-capacity streets. Many roads still were unpaved. In 1946, there were about 100,000 automobiles in Denver alone. By 1959, that number had more than doubled.

Mayor Quigg Newton met the challenge of the automobile by changing the authority for traffic engineering from the police department to a separate Department of Traffic Engineering as part of the Department of Improvement and Parks. To head the department, he hired traffic engineer Henry Barnes. Some of the most innovative solutions to Denver's growing traffic problems during the late 1940s and early 1950s were devised by Barnes. Barnes also set up an alternating one-way street system downtown, converted many residential streets near the central business district to one-way, installed additional street signs and traffic lights, and set up computer-controlled, synchronized signal lights so traffic could "hit the green lights" along a stretch of road if they were traveling at the speed limit.

24) Traffic signals on many of the downtown intersections stop traffic in all directions and allow pedestrians to cross diagonally and without interference from cars. It is called the "Barnes Dance" after traffic engineer Henry Barnes.

25) The dreaded Denver Boot awaits anyone who doesn't pay their parking tickets. The device was invented in Denver in 1955 and immobilizes a car by clamping onto a tire. It is now used around the world.

Outside of the city, more roads were needed to serve the growing metropolitan area. Although an extensive street system had been planned as early as 1928 when the Denver Planning Commission published its "Major Street Plan," little was done until the 1950s. By the middle of the decade, traffic planning focused primarily on creating a system that would link the downtown area with the new suburbs sprouting up around Denver. There were even plans for high-speed mass transit and express bus routes to fringe suburban parking lots, ideas that have just recently been implemented. A 1957 supplement to the *Denver Post* reported that "All the planning is aimed at moving traffic from downtown to the farthest suburbs on major arteries which interlink to form a series of fast-traffic rings around the entire metropolitan area."

This started to become a reality during the war when the Sixth Avenue freeway was laid out from the city to the Denver Ordnance Plant (later the Denver Federal Center) at Kipling Street. Statewide, Colorado imposed a two-cent-per-gallon tax on gasoline to match federal funds, which allowed the state to receive road construction money made possible by the Federal Highway Act of 1944. In 1952, the Denver-Boulder

26) *The Valley Highway was the first major freeway through the center of the city. Officially designated Interstate 25, the highway has been widened many times since its completion in 1958, but is becoming more crowded, especially at rush hours.*

Turnpike was opened. Commuters paid 25 cents to travel between the two cities or to stop off at the expanding towns of Broomfield or Westminster. The cost of the freeway was paid off in 1967, and the tollbooths at the Broomfield exit were removed.

Within the city limits, the Valley Highway was finally opened in November 1958 after ten years of construction. The expressway followed the course of the Platte River through much of the northern half of the city and was largely built on tax-delinquent land that George Cranmer had acquired during the depression. Enlarged many times since and now designated as Interstate 25, the freeway serves as the main north-south artery through the center of Denver.

To provide an east-west freeway and linkup with the nation's interstate highway system, I-70 was constructed along the northern edge of the city. When it opened in 1966, the highway had been a subject of intense controversy because the freeway cut a wide swath through many residential neighborhoods in northwest Denver and created a noisy, uninviting edge to Rocky Mountain Lake Park and Berkeley Park.

27) As Denver's population has grown so has its highway system, many times to the detriment of neighborhoods. Interstate 70 cut through many residential neighborhoods and parks when it was built in the mid-1960s. (Courtesy of Colorado Department of Transportation; Photo by Philip B. Demosthenes)

28) In 1950, the steel-wheeled trolleys that received their power from overhead wires made their last run. They were replaced by rubber-tired, diesel-powered buses. In 1994, light-rail vehicles were once again introduced to Denver streets when the Metro Area Connection started service. (Courtesy of Regional Transportation District)

Before the number of cars started to explode after the war, most people still rode the trolleys as they had since the turn of the century. In 1945, 111 million people used the transit system of the Denver Tramway Company. Miles of tracks crisscrossed the city. Some rubber-tired electric coaches were introduced in the 1940s and early 1950s. Eventually, buses started to replace trolleys in the late 1940s. The yellow Denver trolleys that ran on steel tracks made their final runs on June 3, 1950, and by 1955 the entire system was converted to diesel buses. With the growth of highways and automobile registration, bus ridership had dropped to 40 million by 1960 and to only 18 million in 1970.

The Denver Tramway Company went out of business in 1970 when the city bought the company for $6.2 million and operated it as Denver Metro Transit. In September 1973, voters in Adams, Arapahoe, Boulder, Denver, and Jefferson counties approved a ½% sales tax to finance a new Regional Transportation District (RTD), which was supposed to coordinate mass transportation throughout the metropolitan area, not just in Denver. On July 4, 1974, RTD assumed operation of Denver Metro Transit.

As Denverites were finding it easier to get around the metropolitan area on wheels, they were finding easier and faster ways to travel and ship merchandise to other parts of the country by airplane. Eugene Cervi predicted as early as 1945 in the October 11 issue of the *Rocky Mountain Journal* that "Denver will flourish as an air center. Products can be shipped out by air, making manufacturing profitable."

Stapleton Airfield had been a quiet airstrip since its opening in 1929 with little growth during the depression and World War II. After 1945, things began to change with the increasing population and technological improvements in airplanes made during the war. In 1946, only 249,729 passengers traveled into and out of Denver. By 1956, that number had grown to 624,555 passengers, and by 1958, more than 1.5 million passengers used the airfield. Air freight increased from 1.3 million pounds in 1946 to 11.8 million pounds in 1956.

Denver became home to some major airlines. United Airlines had been formed before the war in 1934, but in 1948 made Denver its operational base and still maintains major hub service at Denver International Airport. Continental Airlines also had been formed before the war in

29) *The United Airlines Flight Center was opened in August 1968 adjacent to Stapleton International Airport. It includes classrooms, flight simulators, and offices. The 289,000 square foot facility cost $7.5 million to build and was initially outfitted with $22.5 million worth of equipment.*

1939 when Robert Six consolidated several smaller carriers. Monarch Airlines was formed in 1946, but in 1950 Monarch became Frontier Airlines when it merged with Challenger Airlines and Arizona Airways. Frontier went bankrupt and eventually became part of Continental Airlines in 1986. A group of former company officials resurrected it in July 1994 when they began flying four flights a day to North Dakota. Trans-World Airlines obtained Denver routes in 1956.

To accommodate the increasing passenger and freight traffic, Stapleton Airfield was expanded and remodeled many times. In the late 1950s the city acquired 400 surplus acres from the Rocky Mountain Arsenal for development of the north-south runway, which was finished in 1959. Additional expansion of the runway occurred in 1969. The name was changed to Stapleton International Airport in 1964. By 1970, 7.4 million passengers were arriving, departing, or making connections at Stapleton annually.

30). Stapleton International Airport, named after Denver's longest term mayor, Benjamin Stapleton, served the city for 64 years. It was expanded many times during that period. It was closed in 1995 when the new Denver International Airport opened. This photograph shows Stapleton in 1980 before concourse E was constructed. (Courtesy of Colorado Department of Transportation; Photo by Philip B. Demosthenes)

Suburban Growth

With the end of the war, the population of the metropolitan area soared. During this boom cycle, however, most of the growth was in the suburbs. Denver grew by about 18% during the 1940s while the surrounding suburban areas grew by 29%. To accommodate the new arrivals, housing developments spread out in all directions, aided by the post-war home-loan programs of the Veterans Administration (VA) and the Federal Housing Authority (FHA).

Between 1950 and 1957, Denver's population grew by 39%, while Aurora grew by 215%, Arvada by 334%, Littleton by 152%, and Westminster by 380%. By 1957, Denver ranked as the third-fastest-growing metropolitan area in the United States, behind Houston and San Diego.

31) Post-war suburban growth exploded during the 1950s and has not slowed down since. New housing developments expanded in every direction. By 1960, the population of the four metropolitan counties of Adams, Arapahoe, Denver, and Jefferson had reached 855,131. By 1970, it was nearly 1.1 million. (The Denver Public Library, Western History Department)

Growing right along with housing development was the new idea of the shopping center. Until shortly after the war, downtown remained the primary shopping district. For daily needs like food, people went to small, neighborhood stores. Shopping patterns began to change in 1951 when the Merchants Park Shopping center opened at 601 South Broadway, built on the site of the old Merchants Park baseball stadium. As the city's first shopping center, it boasted 14 stores with 140,000 square feet of selling space.

Four years later, architect Temple Buell opened the Cherry Creek shopping center at the intersection of First Avenue and University Boulevard. Unlike Merchants Park, the stores at Cherry Creek surrounded a landscaped area that was completely separate from the parking. This was a first for Denver and for much of the rest of the country, and became the style for shopping centers that followed. In Denver these included the Lakeside Mall in the northwest part of town, built in 1956; the Perl-Mack

32) The 1955 Cherry Creek Shopping Center at First Avenue and University Boulevard was one of the first shopping centers in the country and the first in Denver to feature a car-free landscaped area surrounded by anchor stores and smaller shops. (The Denver Public Library, Western History Department)

center north of the city; and the JCRS Shopping Center, built in 1957 on part of the grounds of the Jewish Consumptive Relief Society tuberculosis sanatorium and research center.

By 1957, 25 shopping areas ringed the city with 14 more under construction or in the planning stages. All of them featured from 20 to 50 stores. As the years passed, the centers got larger and larger, like the huge Cinderella City Shopping Center completed in 1968 in Englewood.

Offices also began moving to the suburbs. One of the first major business park developments was the Denver Tech Center. It was started in 1962 by George Wallace, who predicted that the problems with traffic and parking in the downtown area would only get worse as the city grew. Anticipating that the city would grow southeast, he bought farmland along Interstate 25 and began development of a complex of low office buildings set on heavily landscaped grounds with a well-planned system of roads and parking areas. By 1975, the Tech Center had grown to 27 buildings on about 800 acres of land. The Tech Center showed that businesses in a location far away from downtown could work and provide amenities not possible in the central city. It fueled the rapid growth of the southeast part of the metropolitan area and served as a model for the dozens of office parks that followed.

33) *When the Denver Tech Center was first opened in 1962, many people thought it was too far from downtown to be successful. Today, the southeast suburban area is one of the major employment centers in the metropolitan area with office parks and residential developments stretching miles farther south from the original Tech Center. (Courtesy of Colorado Department of Transportation; Photo by Philip B. Demosthenes)*

Cultural and Educational Development

After the war, Denver's cultural and educational institutions began to catch up with the population growth. The Denver Art Museum had languished since the 1934 agreement that had made the Art Museum a department of the City and County of Denver. Part of the agreement provided that the city acquire land for a new building near the Civic Center, while the museum was to begin establishing a building fund. In the late 1940s, some old buildings were purchased at 14th Avenue and Acoma Street, and remodeled during the 1950s to house the expanding collections.

By 1960, the Denver Art Museum was a patchwork facility with limited space for its collection. Otto Karl Bach, director of the museum since 1944, had been experimenting with display techniques and exhibit space design, but he needed more space to make his ideas reality. In 1963, the Board of Directors began studying the needs of the museum and how a new facility could be financed and built. Ultimately, the Italian architect, Gio Ponti, was selected as designer in association with architect James Sudler of Denver.

34) From 1949 until demolition began for the new building in the late 1960s, the Denver Art Museum was housed in a remodeled automobile showroom and other recycled buildings on 14th Avenue across from the Civic Center. (Courtesy of Denver Art Museum)

To accommodate all the required gallery and administrative space on the site of the existing museum, two 10,000 square foot towers were required, along with about 100,000 square feet of additional floor space. Combined with the requirement that there be very few windows to avoid light damage to the art work, the resulting plan produced what Sudler called the appearance of "two immense refrigerators."

The architects modified the brutal mass by adding facets to the basic form and wrapping the large volumes with a skin consisting of sides of interesting proportions. They added some carefully placed windows to help the design of each facade as well as to provide occasional relief with spectacular views of the city skyline, Civic Center, and the Rocky Mountains. The surface was covered with a special ceramic tile developed by the Corning Company especially for the museum building. There are about one million tiles on the building, each one hand-placed on the concrete structural walls.

35) *The design of the Denver Art Museum has been controversial since its completion. Designed by Gio Ponti, its multi-faceted gray tiles glisten in the sun and complement the earlier gray granite used in older buildings around the Civic Center.*

After a successful fund-raising campaign, city officials broke ground for the Denver Art Museum in January 1968. The $6.3 million building was formally opened to the public on October 3, 1971.

Across the street from the art museum to the north, on the Civic Center grounds, the Denver Public Library had been serving Denver readers since 1910. Like the early museum buildings, it was outdated and overcrowded. Although voters approved a bond issue for construction funds in 1947, lack of money for site acquisition and political feuding postponed groundbreaking until August 1954. Some of the money needed to buy the site at 14th and Broadway was raised by selling the old neoclassical structure to the city for municipal offices.

The city selected Burhnam Hoyt as architect, but because he was in ill health he associated with the firm of Fisher and Fisher to carry on much of the work. John Eastlick, the city librarian at the time, wanted the planning of the library to be based on a central service core surrounded by the book stacks and reading area. The main entrance was placed in a rotunda facing the Civic Center. The large expanse of glass enclosing the rotunda was intended to give a clear view of the lobby and tempt the passer-by to come in and browse.

36) *The glass-enclosed rotunda of the Denver Public Library extends toward the Civic Center, and the upper floors step back to avoid blocking off sunlight. The original 1955 building was remodeled as part of new construction that added a seven-story addition on the south side in 1994.*

To transfer 600,000 books and 800,000 documents to the new building, Eastlick devised an unusual solution. He set up a system of conveyor belts from the windows of the old building, across the lawn of the Civic Center, over 14th Avenue, and into the rotunda of the new library. At a cost of about $8,000, the conveyor system worked and the move was completed in about one week. With the book move completed, formal dedication of the library was held on October 16, 1956.

The south wall of the building was kept simple in anticipation of a future addition. It was enclosed in brick that could be removed without harming the structural integrity of the building. The addition finally came to fruition in 1995 when the new building was opened and the existing structure remodeled.

For performing arts entertainment after the war, people attended the Denver Symphony Orchestra and the Bonfils Theater. The Denver Symphony had been formed in 1934 after several earlier incarnations. In 1945, Saul Caston became the conductor. He was followed by Vladimir Golschmann in 1963, who was succeeded by Brian Priestman in 1968. The orchestra performed in the Auditorium Theater created by remodeling the old City Auditorium. The orchestra moved to the new Boettcher Concert Hall in 1978.

The Bonfils Theater opened in October 1953 at East Colfax and Elizabeth Street. It was built for the Denver Civic Theater and paid for by Miss Helen Bonfils in memory of her father, Frederick G. Bonfils, co-founder of the *Denver Post*. With 550 seats, it was considered one of the finest theaters of its type in America.

37) The Bonfils Memorial Theater was a popular attraction from its opening in 1953. As the Denver Performing Arts Complex was developed in the early 1980s, theatrical activity at the Bonfils Memorial Theater was phased out until it closed in 1986. Shortly before it closed, it was renamed the Lowenstein Theater after Henry Lowenstein, who had been a designer and producer at the theater since 1956.

In 1950, the Denver Zoological Gardens Foundation was formed to improve the existing City Park zoo, started in 1918. The Foundation restored the monkey island, the elephant house, and the feline house through the 1950s and 1960s.

Nearby, the Denver Museum of Natural History was enlarged in 1968 to include Gates Planetarium on the west side of the museum. The IMAX theater opened on July 1, 1983 in what was formerly Phipps Auditorium.

Closer to downtown, post-war development included creation of the Denver Botanic Gardens. During mayor Quigg Newton's administration, the city acquired the land between Cheesman and Congress Parks from the Catholic Archdiocese of Denver, which was using it for the Calvary Cemetery. In partial exchange for the site, the city moved all the corpses to Mount Olivet Cemetery in 1950. Initial work then began on an extensive layout of gardens. A conservatory was opened in January 1966 and an education building was completed in March 1971. Major reconstruction of the planting areas began in 1970, and the gardens are now a favorite destination point for both tourists and residents.

Both public and private schools struggled to keep up with the post-war growth. In Denver alone, 55 schools were built between 1945 and 1973, when enrollment rose from 46,682 to 85,438, peaking in 1968 at 96,848. Elementary schools were built first. Most were two-story, horizontal designs typical of the 1950s style of architecture.

Following the aging of the baby boomers, nine junior high schools were built after the war and prior to 1973. These included Grant, Merrill, and Kepner in 1953, Hill (1956), Baker (1957), Kunsmiller (1957),

38) *The Museum of Natural History is still in its prominent location in City Park where it has stood since 1908. The museum added additional exhibition space and the Gates Planetarium in 1968. An IMAX theater was added in 1983.*

Rishel (1959), Hamilton (1969), and Place (1971). High schools were built equally as fast. Manual High was completed in 1953, and Lincoln, Jefferson, and Washington high schools in 1960. Kennedy High School was opened in 1966.

School enrollment began to decline after 1969. Some of the drop was due to the graduation of the first group of baby boom children. Much of the decline, however, was attributed to court-ordered busing of children to achieve racial segregation of the Denver Public Schools. The controversy started when many in the black community saw schools becoming predominantly segregated due to housing patterns and the Denver Public School policy that allowed white families to send their children either to local schools or elsewhere. At first, the school board tried to tackle the problem by setting up a voluntary busing plan in 1969, but the political makeup of the board prevented the plan from doing much good.

The issue finally ended up in Federal District Court and ultimately in the U. S. Supreme Court. In 1974, boundaries were rearranged and pairs of schools were set up for a massive busing effort. Many parents opposed to the plan began moving out of Denver or sending their children to private schools. By 1977, enrollment had dropped to just more than 70,000 students.

New colleges also grew. The extension center of the University of Colorado moved out of its small space at 1405 Glenarm Place to new quarters at 14th and Arapahoe for the start of the fall 1957 semester. During the 1956-57 school year, there were 7,000 students.

39) The Auraria Higher Education Complex opened in January 1977. Some of the oldest neighborhoods in Denver were razed to make way for the shared facilities for the University of Colorado at Denver, Metropolitan State College, and Community College of Denver.

40) By 1970, Denver was beginning to look like a large city. New construction began to dwarf the venerable Daniels and Fisher tower. The Platte Valley still was dominated by railroad yards and industrial buildings, and the Auraria Educational Complex had not yet been built. (Courtesy of Denver Public Library, Western History Department; Photo by E. M. Clark & Associates)

In November 1969, voters approved the city's share of the urban renewal project that became the Auraria Higher Education Center. Located on the west side of Speer Boulevard between Market Street and Colfax Avenue, Auraria was designed as a commuter campus combining the University of Colorado at Denver, Community College of Denver, and Metropolitan State College. Each school maintained its own identity, but shared common facilities such as the library, student center, athletic fields, and gymnasium.

In the suburbs, Red Rocks Community College opened in 1969, and Arapahoe Community College in Littleton started its operation in 1974. Instead of building standard campuses of individual buildings, both community colleges originally housed all facilities in a single building.

When Eugene Cervi died in 1970, Denver and Colorado had come of age. Many of the predictions he had made after the war had come true. Denver was no longer a sleepy, isolated prairie town. The population had soared, new industries were established, a new skyline pierced the clouds, a network of roads and highways connected the new suburbs, and educational and cultural opportunities abounded. And Denver was still a beautiful place to live.

PART FIVE

21st-Century Boom Town: 1973 to present

In 1973, one event occurred that changed Denver forever. Like the discovery of gold in 1858, this event involved riches from the earth. Only this time oil was the source of the wealth, and instead of being discovered it was withheld. In retaliation for United States support of Israel, the Arab oil-producing countries moved to embargo shipments of oil to the United States, western Europe, and Japan.

The effect was almost immediate. Gasoline lines formed at service stations as oil prices soared from a little more than $2 per barrel to more than $12 a barrel by the late 1970s. Additional unrest in the Middle East in 1979 caused prices to triple by 1981. Amid the uncertainty of oil supply and price increases, the United States rushed to find additional supplies of energy.

Denver was ideally situated to benefit from the energy crisis. It was centrally located in the Rocky Mountain region that is a source of oil, natural gas, coal, and oil shale. In addition, Denver is one of the sunniest places in the country, making it ideal for the research and application of solar energy.

Growth in the '70s and '80s

One of the first visible effects of the energy crisis was the explosion of office buildings in Denver and surrounding counties to house the new and expanding oil and gas companies and all the support services they required. New construction was slow in the early 1970s due to tight money. Most downtown construction was financed by local investors or insurance companies. In 1970, Denver's population had peaked at 514,678 while the metropolitan area (including Denver) was home to 1,229,866 people. By 1980, Denver's population dropped to 492,365 and the metro area's population grew to 1,593,308.

By 1976, a new building boom had started, financed by money from Canada, Europe, and Hawaii as well as by mainland U.S. investors. Between 1973 and 1979, nine major downtown office projects were built, adding more than 4 million square feet of office space. These included the 410 Building, the Anaconda Tower, and Energy Center One (later renamed to the Petro-Lewis Tower and now Manville Plaza) all completed in 1978, and the aluminum-clad Amoco Building at the head of 17th Street, completed in 1980.

1) Much of today's downtown skyline is a result of the building boom in the late 1970s and early 1980s. During that time, energy companies and related services created an unprecedented demand for office space.

The real explosion of office towers occurred in the early 1980s, both downtown and in suburban office parks. Much of the new development was financed by Canadian firms. A *Denver Post* survey in 1981 identified 24 separate Canadian land investment and development companies active in the Denver metropolitan area. Their combined investment was almost $1 billion in office buildings, apartments, and shopping centers.

Outside of the downtown area, 20 business parks were developed in the suburbs between 1981 and 1982. Most of the growth was along the Interstate 25 corridor in the southeast portion of the metro area. In 1981, the Denver Tech Center had grown to 850 acres with about 2.5 million square feet of office space. Across I-25, developer John Madden built Greenwood Plaza. Started in 1970, Madden's development had grown to 3 million square feet of office space by 1981 with an additional 11 buildings under construction. That same year, Madden announced more development on the 80-acre tract of Greenwood Plaza South.

Farther south along I-25, Inverness Business Park leased more than 2 million square feet in 1981 with another half million under construction. Inverness also sported an 18-hole golf course.

Between 1980 and 1983, about 31 million square feet of office space became available in the metropolitan area, compared to only 7.6 million for the five years from 1975 to 1979. In the downtown area alone, about 11.5 million square feet of office space was added by major projects. Downtown lease rates for office space shot up 144% between 1978 and 1982, while those in the southeast corridor along I-25 rose by about 125%. Downtown office vacancy rates stood at an incredibly low 0.1% in mid-1981.

However, as quickly as the building boom had lured investors from all over the world, the bubble burst quickly. As the national recession began to hit Denver in 1982, land speculators and Canadian developers pulled out. Office space that was either committed or under construction resulted in an oversupply as energy companies began to cut back their operations. Offices sat empty. Lease rates that had been in the $22 to $24 per square foot range in late 1981 dropped to $15 to $17 in early 1983.

The Republic Plaza Building and the One Tabor Center building, both completed in 1984, and the 1999 Broadway Building, completed in 1985, were the last of the large downtown office towers built during the construction frenzy of the early 1980s.

Much of the new downtown construction took place in the Skyline Urban Renewal Project. Skyline was just one of the many projects of the Denver Urban Renewal Authority (DURA). Other DURA projects included Blake and Jerome parks; two industrial developments, Mitchell and Whittier; two residential areas; and the Avondale project east of Federal Boulevard along Colfax Avenue.

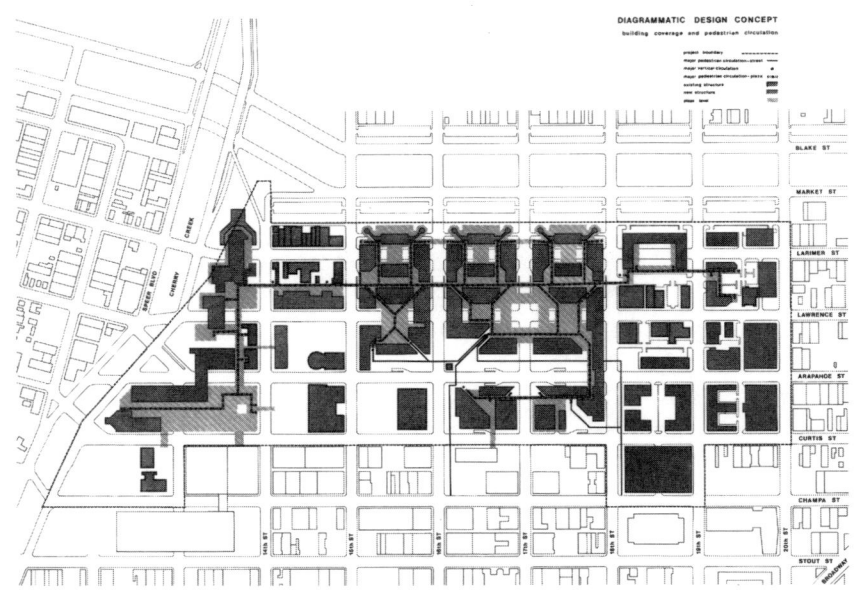

2) The original Skyline urban design plan envisioned separating pedestrian traffic from vehicle traffic with a system of second-level pedestrian plazas connected with bridges over the streets. Only a few of the second-level plazas have been built.

Skyline was DURA's most visible project and one of the most controversial. The Skyline project was a 27-block area stretching from Speer Boulevard to 20th Street and from the alley between Market and Larimer to Curtis Street. Voter approval for the project occurred in 1967, and initial planning and drafting of an urban design development plan was completed in 1970. By that time, land had been acquired with help from a $33 million federal grant. By 1972, most of the area had been cleared of buildings. Most of the criticism directed at DURA at the time centered on the agency's wholesale destruction of existing buildings, many of them historic structures dating to Denver's earliest days such as the Iron Building (1892), the Federal Reserve Bank Building (1925), and the Tabor Building (1880).

Fortunately, a few projects were started, but at first they were lone structures in a sea of asphalt parking lots. Prudential Plaza (now called Independence Plaza) was the first full-block development planned according to the Skyline design guidelines. Sited between 16th and 17th Street and Arapahoe and Curtis streets, it opened in February 1972 and combined office and retail space. Prudential Plaza included 40% open space, a second-level pedestrian plaza, and was set back 50 feet along 16th Street to maintain an open area south of the Daniels and Fisher tower.

The next year, Park Central was completed. This full-block office complex housed Central Bank, and its slick black exterior fronted on the first phase of Skyline Park, built by DURA along Arapahoe Street on either side of the Daniels and Fisher tower. The two-block extension of the park was not completed until 1977.

Other projects completed in the early 1970s in the Skyline area included the headquarters for Mountain Bell, Dravo Plaza at 14th and Lawrence, a fire station, bus terminal, Sakura Square housing, Sunset Park apartments, and Skyline Park apartments.

The demolition of so many historic structures in the Skyline urban renewal area galvanized the historic preservation movement. The Denver Landmark Preservation Commission had been established in 1967 and Historic Denver in 1970, but not until the leveling of such a large area did a majority of private citizens and public officials realize how quickly Denver could lose symbols of its legacy.

3) Just a few of the bridges originally planned for the Skyline Urban Renewal Project have been built. The second-level pedestrian concept has not proved as popular as the planners envisioned. Just one project, the Tabor Center, actually spans across a street with usable space as originally designed.

In addition to Larimer Square, which already had been developed, few old buildings remained in the Skyline area. The Tramway Cable building had been spared and rehabilitated into a restaurant and offices. The old Daniels and Fisher store fell to the wrecker's ball, but the tower portion remained. It was finally renovated in 1983 into office condominiums and serves as a major focal point in the midtown area.

Farther uptown, sensitivity to historic preservation helped give new life to the Ideal Building at 17th and Champa for Colorado Federal Savings in 1980, the Equitable Building, and the Kittredge Building in 1981. After an arsonist set fire to the Masonic Building on March 4, 1984, it nearly burned to the ground. Only the thick, exterior stone walls remained. Instead of tearing it down, a new structure was built within the walls and it reopened in August 1985.

In lower downtown, a few urban pioneers were beginning to rehabilitate the old buildings just northwest of the Skyline project during the early 1970s. Since that time, the area has become one of the most active and exciting places in the central business district, with a diverse collection of offices, apartments, lofts, restaurants, galleries, nightclubs, and the new Coors baseball field.

4) After the May Company closed the Denver Dry Goods Company in 1987, the building remained vacant for years. It was renovated into retail stores and housing in 1993, and its exterior brick was restored to its original appearance.

5) *The Corona School on Capitol Hill (now known as the Dora Moore School) was built in 1889 and designed by architect Robert S. Roeschlaub. A major addition was added in 1993, and the original building has been renovated.*

The city's emerging sensitivity to its history and natural assets was not confined to buildings. For years the South Platte River through Denver had been a neglected waterway, dumping spot, and haven for the homeless. To clean up the Platte, in 1974 Mayor William H. McNichols, Jr., asked state Senator Joe Shoemaker to chair a Platte River Development Committee. With $1.9 million in seed money from revenue sharing funds, the committee began to construct the Platte River Greenway.

The first project was Confluence Park, the location where Denver began at the point where Cherry Creek flows into the South Platte. It included a footbridge over the Platte, a natural grass amphitheater, and a paved plaza now called Shoemaker Plaza. In 1976, the non-profit South Platte River Foundation was formed to help complete the project.

6) *The Cherry Creek bike trail and the Platte River bike trail converge at Confluence park. The junction of the two rivers marks the birthplace of Denver.*

After seven years and $14 million in additional money from private donations and public funds, the foundation had built a 10.5-mile hiking and bicycle trail from Dartmouth to 52nd Avenue as well as 16 miniparks along the way. The river banks were cleaned up and additional trees planted. Neighboring suburbs added to the trail, which now extends to Chatfield Dam on the south and to 88th Avenue on the north. The Cherry Creek bike trail connects with it at Confluence Park and traverses to Cherry Creek Dam.

As the Platte River trail winds it way through central Denver, it is a small part of the larger redevelopment of the central Platte Valley, the area between the river and Union Station. Once home to railroad yards,

7) *Since the railroad yards have been removed, the Platte River Valley between the river and downtown is one of the largest undeveloped tracts of land in the city. Coors Field and Elitch's Amusement Park were the first major developments in the valley.*

8) *Construction was underway on the roller coaster at the new Elitch Gardens in June 1994. Elitch's moved to the Platte Valley in 1995 after outgrowing its original home in North Denver. The popular Denver attraction anchors the southwest end of the Platte Valley and now provides year-round entertainment.*

warehouses, and industrial sites, the Platte Valley has been the focus of many plans since the 1965 flood. In the mid-1970s, the Burlington Northern Land Development Corporation planned to build a new town in the area, but that scheme never developed. Today, the valley is seen as a destination point for visitors to the city and as a recreation area.

The land has been cleared, railroad tracks removed or relocated, and the area is being redeveloped into new uses. As of 1994, the city of Denver had invested nearly $213 million for improvements in roads and bridges for the 500-acre valley site. On the northeastern edge, Coors Field baseball stadium was completed in time for the 1995 baseball season. Elitch's amusement park moved to an area west of Speer Boulevard in 1995. On the other side of the Platte, near Seventh and Water Street, Colorado Ocean Journey plans to build a $60 million aquarium for a 1996 opening. The 16th Street Mall also will be extended to Union Station. In 1994, the Denver Nuggets basketball team even started discussing a new arena in the valley near Speer Boulevard and Auraria Parkway.

9) *Developers plan to build a $60 million aquarium at Seventh and Water streets in the Platte Valley. The Colorado's Ocean Journey aquatic life park is scheduled to open in 1996.*

Building for the Common Good

A year after the Arab oil embargo, the Poundstone amendment was added to the Colorado Constitution in 1974. Named after Freda J. Poundstone, primary author and supporter of the change, the amendment required that Denver gain countywide voter approval of any proposed annexation in the county that would lose land to the city. This effectively stopped Denver from adding to its tax base while the suburbs reaped the benefits of the exploding growth taking place outside the city limits of Denver. Although the amendment was promoted as a way for the suburbs to keep their tax base, most suburbs were afraid of becoming part of Denver, which at the time was in the thick of court-mandated busing of schoolchildren to achieve racial integration.

Despite the freeze in annexation as a way to expand the tax base, Denver continued to build public facilities and maintain the city's infrastructure. One of the first major additions to the Civic Center area since completion of the art museum came courtesy of the State of Colorado. During the city's growth in the 1960s and 1970s, both the Supreme Court and the Colorado State Museum had outgrown their existing spaces. After several studies and suggestion for a new site, Senator Joe Shoemaker proposed that both the Supreme Court and Colorado State Museum be placed on the block of land across from the Capitol park space, between Broadway and Lincoln streets south of 14th Avenue.

10) Completed in 1977, the judicial/heritage complex houses the Colorado Supreme Court in the block-shaped building facing the Civic Center. The Colorado State Museum is behind it.

After an architectural competition to select the designers for the two buildings, the firm of Rogers, Nagel, Langhart of Denver was selected. They sited the Supreme Court building along 14th Avenue and squeezed the museum into a three story wedge-shaped building, with the majority of the museum underground, on the southern portion of the block. The Judicial/Heritage Center Complex opened on June 1, 1977.

Construction of the 16th Street Mall, one of Denver's most exciting changes, began in April 1980. The mall originally had been proposed as early as 1970 by Downtown Denver, Inc., and the Denver Planning Office. In 1973, C.F. Murphy Associates/Denver was selected to produce a design study. It was completed in 1974, but no progress was made. The mall finally was built as an Urban Mass Transportation Project by the Regional Transportation District (RTD) with money from the U. S. Department of Transportation. Formally named the 16th Street Transitway Mall Project, it was designed to improve transportation in the central business district by providing free shuttle bus service between two bus transportation centers at either end. The final design was developed by the architectural firm of I. M. Pei, and the mall opened on October 7, 1982.

11) The 16th Street Mall is one of downtown Denver's favorite gathering spots. Several restaurants have outdoor dining along the mall, and free shuttle buses carry workers and visitors along its length. The mall opened in 1982.

181

The pleasant day the mall opened gave no indication of what was to come, both meteorologically or politically. On December 24, 1982, Denver received one of its worst snowstorms ever. In a little more than a 24-hour period the day before Christmas, the city was buried under two feet of snow. Most of the city was paralyzed, as was Stapleton Airport. Travel plans were canceled; the newspapers didn't publish. Instead of driving, many people skied along city streets.

It took days to get the city back to normal, and many residents blamed the poor snow removal effort on Mayor William McNichols. Although not entirely his fault, the voters remembered the blizzard of '82 when they went to the polls the following spring. McNichols had been mayor since 1968 and had administered daily city business adequately, but many people felt new leadership was required. A young state representative, Federico Peña, joined in a four-way election with the mayor, Monte Pasco, and former District Attorney Dale Tooley. After a run-off election with Tooley, Peña won the election by just 4,410 votes. Running on a campaign slogan of "Imagine a Great City," Peña struggled through the hard economic times of the mid-1980s, but began laying plans for new city improvements.

12) Rebuilding of the Speer Boulevard viaduct has returned some of the elegance of Mayor Speer's City Beautiful to the long-neglected roadway. The street is a major access route from north Denver into the central business district.

Access to the downtown area was improved during the 1980s with several viaduct and street projects. In 1983, the dilapidated Colfax Viaduct was demolished and rebuilt in 1984. The 15th Street Viaduct was torn down in 1991 and replaced with a surface road and underpass below train tracks. The old Speer Boulevard Viaduct was completely rebuilt in the early 1990s and enhanced with lawns, new tree planting, lights, and balustrades. New viaducts and access roads from I-25 were under construction in 1994 as part of the high-occupancy vehicle project along the interstate as well as to provide easier access to the new Coors baseball field. These replaced the 20th and 23rd street viaducts. One of the last of the old raised roadways from Highlands, the 16th Street Viaduct, was razed in February 1994.

Despite the new roads and bridge projects, traffic problems continued to plague the metropolitan area in 1993. That year, the number of vehicles nearly outnumbered the number of people in the state with 1.4 registered vehicles for every licensed driver; a rate higher than California.

Denver finally got its first fixed rail mass transportation system in the fall of 1994. The first phase of the Regional Transportation District's Metro Area Connection (MAC) connected transfer points at both ends of the line at I-25 and Broadway, and 30th and Downing streets. Bus riders will transfer from these points to take the light rail system downtown. RTD estimated that the new system would take 525 buses off the downtown streets.

13) *After several unsuccessful attempts to build mass transit during the 1970s and 1980s, RTD's solution to transportation problems focused on the use of buses. Park-and-ride facilities were built on the outskirts of the city, with express buses taking commuters downtown.*

14) Opened as a demonstration project in the fall of 1994, the Metro Area Connection (MAC) light rail project was designed to take commuters from one of two express bus transfer stations into the central business district. If it is successful, additional lines may be extended to other parts of the city.

At the beginning of 1980, Currigan Hall convention center was beginning to show its age and was inadequate for larger conventions. The city began studying sites for a new convention center in 1982 including one at Union Station, one two blocks southeast of Currigan, one expanding Currigan Hall and incorporating the Auditorium Arena, and one adjacent to the existing center. After many years, several more studies, and much controversy, a site was selected across Champa Street stretching

15) Architectural critics complained about the design of the Colorado Convention Center when it opened, but it has made it possible for Denver to attract major conventions.

from 14th Street to Speer Boulevard. The $126 million Colorado Convention Center opened in spring 1990 and contained almost one million square feet of space.

The same year the convention center opened, voters in Denver approved a bond issue for $90 million to build a new central library, branch libraries, and renovate several existing branch libraries. The majority of the money, $64 million, was to be used to build a much-needed central library to replace the overcrowded facility.

To select an architect, the city held a competition in 1991 and from three finalists selected Michael Graves of Princeton, New Jersey, with the Denver firm of Klipp Colussy Jenks DuBois. The controversial design retains the classic 1956 structure designed by Burnham Hoyt. The new 540,000 square foot library addition is seven stories high, and the entire project was to be completed by mid-1995.

16) Construction was on schedule in June 1994 for the Central Library of the Denver Public Library system. The addition was scheduled for completion in March 1995, with the remodeling of the existing facility to be complete by early summer 1995.

By far, the most significant construction project for the metropolitan area in the early 1990s was Denver International Airport. The need for a new airport to replace Stapleton was raised as early as 1974 by the Federal Aviation Agency and the Denver Regional Council of Governments. At the time, most people thought that future needs could be met by expanding onto land of the Rocky Mountain Arsenal. Newly elected Mayor Federico Peña's first choice was for expansion. However, Adams county officials moved to block the expansion.

After nearly a year of study, discussion, and negotiation between Denver and Adams county officials, the two counties announced in January 1985 that a new airport should be built on land east of the Rocky Mountain Arsenal. While additional planning and studies were proceeding, the airlines kept growing while Denver grew in importance as a national hub. In 1986, 34 million passengers passed through Stapleton and planners predicted growth to continue into the next decade.

In January 1988, Denver and Adams counties agreed on a 53-square mile site for the new airport, and in May of that year Adams county voters approved Denver's annexation of the land. During the time, there was considerable controversy over whether Denver needed such a large airport, where it should be located, and what the cost should be. In a referendum vote on May 16, 1989, Denver residents approved the new airport idea by a margin of nearly two to one. Three months later, the FAA approved the environmental impact statement, and on September 28, 1989, ground was broken for what was to be the largest public works project in the country.

Construction proceeded rapidly for a project of its size. Although the opening date was postponed four times because of problems with the complex automated baggage system, the airport was to begin operation in 1995; its cost, about $4.2 billion, according to General Accounting Office estimates in November 1994.

The most noticeable aspect of DIA, besides its vast size, is the tent-shaped roof of the main terminal building. The roof is Teflon-coated fiberglass weighing only one and a half pounds per square foot. It is supported by 34 steel masts and is translucent enough to let in natural light during the day and glow from the interior lighting at night. An underground train takes passengers from the main terminal to one of three remote concourses.

The airport was to open with five runways, 88 active gates, and the tallest control tower in the world at 327 feet. However, there is enough room for 12 runways, two more passenger concourses, and another terminal building of the same size as the first. One of the most controversial aspects of the project and the one that caused several delays in opening is an automated baggage-handling system that would transport individual pieces of luggage in small carts along 21 miles of track and 5.7 miles of conveyor belts.

By the time Denver International Airport was to open, the airline industry had changed. Every airline was looking for ways to save money and survive. Even the viability of the hub system was being questioned. Locally, Continental Airlines was cutting back operations through Denver and its long term presence in Denver as a hub airport was being questioned. The bonds that were sold to finance most of the airport are to be paid back by the airlines through increased landing fees. However, higher landing fees are passed on to the passengers, which will make it difficult for the airlines to operate profitably out of the new Denver airport.

As with the original Stapleton airfield, only time will tell if the new airport will be a folly or will keep Denver as a major hub of the world's transportation system.

17) The main terminal building at Denver International Airport is covered with a fabric roof inspired by the Rocky Mountains and designed to give the traveler a memorable impression of Denver. (Courtesy of Denver International Airport)

Economic Boom and Bust

The massive size of the new airport as a construction project was supposed to help revitalize the area's lagging economy. Since the Arab oil embargo, Denver's economy followed its historical cycle of boom and bust. The good times of the late 1970s and early 1980s gave way to the recession of the late 1980s. In addition to cutbacks in the oil and gas industry, other businesses, like the electronics, began to lay off employees and cut back on production. By 1989, bankruptcies had grown to an all-time high. Many businesses failed, office vacancy rates remained high, and home prices declined.

As the 1990s began, things were turning around. More people than ever were moving to Colorado from other states, most notably California and Texas. The oil and gas industry stabilized, mining companies like Newmont Mining and Cyprus Mineral Company were growing, and the cable television industry continued to expand its operations.

18) The Denver Tech Center and other office parks in the southeast part of the metro area are home to dozens of major corporations and smaller businesses. The southeast area has as much office space as downtown Denver.

19) Jones Intercable is one of many cable television companies that is headquartered in the metropolitan area, making Denver what many consider the center of the cable television industry.

Denver is the center of the cable television industry. It began in the early 1950s when Bill Daniels set up a cable television system in Casper, Wyoming, and later moved to Denver. In late 1960, Bob Magness headquartered the predecessor of Tele-Communications Incorporated (TCI) in Denver. Others followed, and today the metropolitan area is home to such giants as TCI, Jones Intercable, Inc., and American Television & Communications Corporation. Just as mining and railroads had made millionaires a century before, by 1993 seven of Colorado's 50 richest people had made their fortunes in cable television.

20) The Rocky Mountain News publishes from its new building on West Colfax Avenue. The newspaper was established by William Byers and printed its first edition on April 23, 1859.

With the growth of business and other activity in Colorado, the daily and weekly newspapers have followed the action. *The Rocky Mountain News*, publishing since 1859, completed its move to its new headquarters in 1992. Denver's other major daily, *The Denver Post*, ran out of room at its headquarters at 15th and California and moved into a high-rise building adjacent to the Civic Center in 1989. Its printing operations had been moved to a plant near I-25 and I-70 in September 1986. Weekly papers, like *Westword*, offer an alternative view to happenings in the metropolitan area.

Housing developments have followed the general economic cycle and have spread in all four directions from Denver. In 1981, Mission Viejo of California, a subsidiary of Philip Morris, Inc., began the huge Highlands Ranch development south of County Line Road, stretching from I-25 west to Santa Fe Drive. Today, it is one of the largest residential developments in the metropolitan area. It is in Douglas County, which in 1994 was the fastest-growing county in the country.

21) *In the latter part of the 1980s and early 1990s, the Highlands Ranch development south of the city exploded with houses. It is typical of the continued suburban growth of the Denver metropolitan area.*

Cultural and Educational Expansion

Cultural and educational institutions also have grown in the past two decades. The Denver Center for the Performing Arts was under construction in the late 1970s and utilized the existing auditorium theater and auditorium arena. Three structures were built—a concert hall, a theater, and a parking garage—and were connected to the existing structure with a glass-topped atrium.

The Boettcher Concert Hall opened on March 4, 1978, and the Helen Bonfils Theater complex opened on December 31, 1980. When it opened, the Theater building contained three smaller theaters in addition to the main theater. In October 1991, the Temple Hoyne Buell Theater was opened. It was constructed in the shell of the old auditorium arena. The auditorium theater also was remodeled and, on the outside, Mayor Speer's auditorium was restored to much of its original appearance.

Today the Denver Performing Arts Complex is home to the Colorado Symphony, the Colorado Ballet, the Colorado Contemporary Dance, Denver Center Theater Company, Opera Colorado, and Robert Garner Center Attractions. There are nine theaters in the complex, making it the second-largest arts complex in the country after Lincoln Center in New York.

22) *The original 1908 City Auditorium was incorporated into the Denver Center for the Performing Arts. The complex also includes Boettcher Concert Hall, The Denver Center Theater Company complex, and a parking garage.*

23) Conductor Marin Alsop led the Colorado Symphony Orchestra in 1994. The orchestra performs in the 2,650-seat Boettcher Concert Hall, which is the only full-surround concert hall in the United States. Reflecting dishes can be lowered or raised to change acoustics. The Colorado Symphony is an outgrowth of the former Denver Symphony Orchestra, which was dissolved in 1989 after financial difficulties and labor-management problems. (Courtesy of Colorado Symphony Orchestra)

Other popular performing arts organizations include the Arvada Center for the Arts and Humanities, the Denver Civic Theater, the Aurora Fox Arts Center, the University of Denver theater, and the Changing Scene, among others.

All of the cultural facilities in the Denver metropolitan area got a boost in 1988 when the cultural facilities tax was approved by voters in Adams, Arapahoe, Boulder, Denver, Douglas and Jefferson counties. The tax, which amounts to a 0.1% sales tax, is divided among large and small cultural facilities in the Cultural Facilities District such as the Zoo, the Denver Art Museum, the Children's Museum, and other groups.

The Denver Art Museum and the Museum of Natural History continue to expand. The Art Museum completed a major renovation for its 100th anniversary in 1993 and has moved some of its administration space to other buildings to free up more gallery space for exhibits. It is part of the Civic Center Cultural Complex, which also includes the Denver Central Library and the Colorado Historical Society. The group has developed a master plan to connect the facilities along 13th Avenue with a park.

24) The original buildings of the Museum of Natural History are now enclosed with new construction after a 1987 addition, and the dinosaur bones remain an attraction. The museum started charging admission in 1982, but it is still a popular destination for both residents and visitors.

In the spring of 1987, the Museum of Natural History added 200,000 square feet of space to its existing 200,000 square feet and remodeled many of its older exhibit spaces. It is now the fifth largest natural history museum in the country. Although it began to charge admission in 1982, it is still one of the city's most popular attractions.

After many years of financial problems and labor disputes, the Denver Symphony Orchestra was dissolved in 1989. The musicians reorganized it as the Colorado Symphony Orchestra (CSO) and now run the popular orchestra. While still struggling with finances, attendance was up 32% in 1994 and ticket revenue was up by 12% the same year. The CSO performs pop concerts, summer concerts, and school programs, as well as a traditional concert series.

Denver is home to several post-secondary schools. Three schools share the campus and many facilities of the Auraria Higher Education Center. Located just west of the central business district, Auraria includes the University of Colorado at Denver, Community College of Denver, and

25) The University of Colorado Health Sciences Center includes the University's School of Medicine, University Hospital, and numerous research centers. The hospital is operated by the University of Colorado, and the entire center is one of the premier research, teaching, and treatment facilities in the country.

Metropolitan State College of Denver. Other Denver colleges include the University of Denver, founded in 1964, Regis University, and Teikyo-Loretto Heights University, one of five Teikyo University locations in the United States. Within the metropolitan area are Arapahoe Community College, founded in 1965; Colorado School of Mines, organized in 1874; Community College of Aurora, established in 1983; Front Range Community College in Westminster, started in 1985; and Red Rocks Community College, which was founded in Lakewood in 1969. Additional trade schools, private schools, and adult education schools round out a wide variety of educational opportunities.

26) A one-block section of early Denver homes was converted into the Ninth Street Park Historic District on the Auraria campus. The Victorian houses were renovated into administrative offices for the college, and Ninth Street was turned into a grassed area.

Sports Mania

While Denver maintains a status as a highly educated city, it is also a city of sports fans. Sports teams were playing before the turn of the century, and today Denver boasts major league teams in football, baseball, and basketball.

The Denver Broncos football team began play in 1960, but gained its greatest popularity in 1977 when it went to its first Super Bowl. Since then, the team has participated in four Super Bowls and was the AFC Champion for four of six seasons between 1986 and 1991.

There have been several ballparks in Denver since the early part of the century, including Merchants Park on South Broadway at Center Avenue. When Bears Stadium was built in 1948, the Denver Bears minor league team entertained baseball fans on a site overlooking downtown Denver. The name was changed in 1985 to the Denver Zephyrs. The stadium was enlarged to 76,000 seats in 1976, with movable east stands to accommodate both baseball and football. The name was changed to Mile High Stadium.

After nearly 50 years of trying to get a major league team, the Colorado Rockies opened its first season in Mile High Stadium before more than

27) Mile High Stadium is built on the site of the old Bears Stadium. Seating 76,000, the field is home to the Denver Broncos and was used by the Colorado Rockies baseball team for its first two seasons until it moved to Coors Field in 1995.

80,000 fans on April 9, 1993. During the first season of the Colorado Rockies, the ball club broke the major league baseball attendance record when nearly 4.5 million fans attended home games, an average of more than 56,000 per game.

The year before the Rockies played its first season, ground was broken on a new stadium, part of which is on the site where the first train arrived in Denver in June 1870 at the Denver Pacific Railway Depot. After playing its first two seasons at Mile High Stadium, the team moved to the new Coors Field in April 1995 for its third season. Coors field was designed along the lines of an "old-time" baseball park in the Platte Valley near 23rd and Blake streets. The $141.5 million ballpark seats about 50,000 fans around an asymmetrical, natural grass field.

Across the street from Mile High Stadium, the Denver Nuggets plays its home games in McNichols Arena. The Nuggets began play in the National Basketball League in 1977 and are another popular sports draw.

Denver is also the site of the annual International Golf Tournament at Castle Pines Golf Club. Started in 1985 by oilman Jack Vickers, the tournament piqued the curiosity of the professional golf world with its unique Stableford scoring system. The format of the tournament has been modified slightly over the years, but still draws the top names in golf as part of the PGA tour.

28) *Originally planned as a venue for the 1976 International Winter Olympics, McNichols Arena is now home to the Denver Nuggets Basketball team and other sporting and entertainment events.*

29) In mid-1994, construction of Coors Field was on schedule for opening in time for the 1995 baseball season. The 50,000-seat stadium will have a brick exterior and is transforming the lower downtown neighborhood around it by encouraging development of restaurants, clubs, housing, and upgrades to streets and other city infrastructure.

For many Denverites, having major league sports indicates Denver itself has made it into the big league. Although the city still retains much of its western heritage, it can no longer be considered a "cow town." Today, Denver is cosmopolitan, diverse, vibrant, and simply beautiful. And today, before and after a football or baseball game, you will still find people enjoying themselves in the restaurants and clubs near where General William Larimer built his cabin, along Larimer Street, "the best" street.

30) Denver's past is maintained at the Buckhorn Exchange at Tenth and Osage streets. In 1893, Henry H. "Shorty Scout" Zietz opened a saloon that catered to railroaders across the street. Shorty ran the Buckhorn until his death in 1949, when his son, Henry, Jr., took over. In 1978, it was sold to a group of Denverites who restored it and moved the bar upstairs. It has a collection of three generations of taxidermy trophies, firearms, photographs, and Indian artifacts, and still operates under the state's liquor license #1.

Sources

Chapman Publishing Company. *Portrait and Biographical Record of Denver and Vicinity*. Chicago: Chapman Publishing Co., 1898.

Adams, Eugene H., Dorsett, Lyle W., and Pulcipher, Robert S. *The Pioneer Western Bank First of Denver: 1860–1980*. Denver: The State Historical Society of Colorado, 1984.

Albi, Charles and Forrest, Kenton. *The Moffat Tunnel: A Brief History*. Golden, Colorado: Colorado Railroad Museum, 1978.

American Sight-Seeing Car & Coach Company. *Seeing Denver*. Denver: The American Sight-Seeing Car & Coach Company, 1903.

Arps, Louisa Ward. *Denver in Slices*. Athens, Ohio: Swallo Press, 1983.

Brettell, Richard R. *Historic Denver: The Architects and the Architecture, 1858–1893*. Denver: Historic Denver, Inc., 1973.

The Denver Post. "This is Colorado," Special Centennial Magazine Section of the *The Denver Post*. *The Denver Post*, June 21, 1959.

The Denver Post. "Denver, A Progress Report of the Greater Denver Area, 1957," supplement to *Empire*, the magazine of *The Denver Post*, vol. 3. *The Denver Post Empire* magazine, 1957.

Dorsett, Lyle W. *The Queen City: A History of Denver*, 2nd ed. Boulder, Colorado: Pruett Publishing Company, 1986.

Fletcher, Ken. *A Mile High & Three Feet Six Wide*. Aurora, Colorado: Mountain West Enterprises, 1993.

Haber, Francine, Fuller, Kenneth R., Wetzel, David N., and Roeschlaub, Robert S. *Architect of the Emerging West*. Denver: Colorado Historical Society, 1988.

Hafen, LeRoy. *Colorado and Its People: Narrative and Topical History of the Centennial State*, vol. 4. New York: Lewis Historical Publishing, 1948.

Halaas, David Fridtjof. *Fairmont and Historic Colorado*. Denver: The Fairmont Cemetery Association, 1976.

Hunt, Corinne. *The Brown Palace Story*, Centennial Edition. Denver: Rocky Mountain Writers Guild, 1982.

Jones, William C., and Forrest, Kenton. *Denver: A Pictoral History*, 3rd ed. Golden, Colorado: Colorado Railroad Museum, 1993.

Kelly, George V. *The Old Gray Mayors of Denver*. Boulder, Colorado: Pruett Publishing Company, 1974.

Larimer, William Henry Harrison. *Reminiscences of General William Larimer and His Son William H.H. Larimer*. Lancaster, Pennsylvania: New Era Printing Company, 1918.

Leonard, S. J. and Noel, T. J. *Denver: Mining Camp to Metropolis*. Niwot, Colorado: University Press of Colorado, 1990.

Leonard, Stephen J. *Trials and Triumphs*. Niwot, Colorado: University Press of Colorado, 1993.

Levy, Michael H., and Scanlan, Staff Sargeant Patrick M. *Pursuit of Excellence: A History of Lowry Air Force Base, 1937–1987*. Denver: History Office, Lowry Technical Training Center, 1987.

McKeever, Gene, Forrest, Kenton, and McAllister, Raymond. *History of the Public Schools of Denver*. Denver: Tramway Press, Inc., 1989.

Noel, T. J. *Richthofen's Montclair*. Denver: Graphic Impressions, Inc., 1976.

Noel, Thomas J., and Norgren, Barbara S. *Denver: The City Beautiful*. Denver: Historic Denver, Inc., 1987.

Picher, Margaret. "Eugene Cervi and Cervi's Rocky Mountain Journal: A Study of Post World War II in Colorado." Ph.D. dissertation, University of Denver, 1986.

Ronzio, Richard A. *Silver Images of Colorado: Denver Album & The 1866 Business Directory*, Vol. 1. Denver: Sundance Publications, Ltd., 1986.

Smiley, Jerome C. *History of Denver*. Denver: The Denver Times, The Times-Sun Publishing Co., 1901.

The Colorado State Planning Commission. *Year Book of the State of Colorado, 1943–1944*. Denver: The Colorado State Planning Commission, 1944.

Wahlberg, Edgar M. *Voices in the Darkness*. Boulder, Colorado: Roberts Rinehart Publishers, 1983.

Wharton, Junius E. *History of The City of Denver From its Earliest Settlement to the Present Time*. Denver: Byers & Dailey, 1866.

Wiberg, Ruth Eloise. *Rediscovering Northwest Denver: Its History, Its People, Its Landmarks*. Denver: Northwest Denver Books, 1976.

Wickens, James F. *Colorado in the Great Depression*. New York: Garland Publishing, Inc., 1979.

Yonce, Frederick J. *The Denver Public Library: 100th Anniversary Celebration*. Denver: The Denver Public Library, 1989.

Index

Adams, William, 117
Agnes Phipps Memorial Sanatorium 124, **128, 132**
Air Force Finance Center, 139
Airline service, 158–160
Airports, 107–108
Aladdin Theater, 78
Allied Architects Association, 112–113
American Television & Communications Corporation, 189
Amoco Building, 172
Amusement parks, 46, 74–77
Anaconda Tower, 172
Annexation, 180
Apollo Hall, 44–45
Arapaho Indians, 2
Arapahoe Community College, 170, 194
Arapahoe County, 7, 50
Arapahoe County Courthouse, 14, **50, 115,** 132, 139
Arapahoe School, 39, **40,** 41
Archer, James, 22, 26
Argo, 22, 36
Argo smelter, 13
Arlington Park, 60, 74
Arnold, Henry, 56
Art galleries, 44
Artesian wells, 23

Arvada Center for the Arts and Humanities, 192
Ashland School, 39
Athenaeum Theater, 45
Auditorium Arena, 147
Auditorium Theater, 147, 167, 191
Auraria, 10, 152
  consolidation with Denver, 9
  founding, 4
Auraria Higher Education Complex, **92,** 101, 152, 154, **169,** 170, 193
Automobiles, 104–105, 143, 155–157

Bach, Karl Otto, 164
Ball Brothers Research Corporation, 145
Ballast, Louis E., 126–127
Bank of Denver, 30
Banks, 27–30, 70–71, 142–143
Barnes Dance, **155**
Barnes, Henry, 155
Barnum, 36
Baseball teams, 195–196
Bears Stadium, 140
Beaver Brook Water Company, 23
Begole, George, 117, 118, 121
Bell, Dr. William A., 20
Benedict, J. B., 113
Bennett, Edward H., 58

Photographs are listed in bold.

201

Berkeley, 50
Berkeley Golf Course, 123
Berkeley Lake, 25
Berkeley neighborhood, 81
Berkeley Park, 60, 157
Bernard, Bella, 51
Blue line, 147–148
Board of Public Works, 49, 59
Board of Supervisors, 47
Boettcher Concert Hall, 167, 191, **192**
Boettcher School for Crippled Children, 122
Boettcher, Charles I, 135, **136**
Boettcher, Charles II, **136**
Boettcher, Claude K., 122, **136**
Bond, N. C., 41
Bonfils Theater, 167
Bonfils, Frederick G., 136, 167
Bonfils, Helen, 167
Boston Building, 14
Botanic Gardens. *See* Denver Botanic Gardens
Bowman, William E., **69**
Brendlinger Block, 12
Breweries, 146
Brick, 11, **12**
Broadway, establishment of, 15
Broadway School, 39
Broadway Theater (performing arts), 45–46
Broadwell Hotel, **9**
Brooks Towers, 70
Brooks, Elwood, 70
Brown's bluff, 16
Brown Mercantile Building, 65
Brown Palace Hotel, **9**, 23, **52, 89**
Brown Palace West Tower, 144
Brown, Henry C., 8–9, 12, 16, 28, 30, 32, 37, 42, 52
Brown, James J., **154**
Brown, Molly, **154**
Buckhorn Exchange, **197**
Bucking Bronco statue, **58**
Buckley Air National Guard Base, 138
Buckley Field, 130
Buell, Temple, 79, 162
Building height limitations, **68**, 138, 153
Bull's Head Corral, 72
Bungalow style house, **81,** 82
Burlington Northern Land Development Corporation, 179

Business district, 12
Business parks, 173
Busing (school), 169
Byers, William, 32, 189
Byers-Evans house, **16**

C. A. Norgren Company, 145
Cable car systems, 37
Cable television companies, 189
Caldwell, Gladys, 124
Calvary Cemetery, 168
Camp George West, 130
Capital Hydraulic Company, 24
Capitol Annex Building, 122
Capitol building, **85, 89, 91**
  completion of, **19**
  construction of, **18**
  gold dome, 19
  interior of, **19, 20**
  site for, 17
Capitol Hill, 15, 99, 152
Capitol Hill pump station, **106**
Carnegie, Andrew, 43
Carter, Edwin, **79**
Castle of Culture and Commerce, 44
Caston, Saul, 167
Cathedral of St. John in the Wilderness, 100
Cathedral of the Immaculate Conception, 100
Cemeteries, **138,** 168
Center Theater, 78
Central Bank, 175
Central Bank and Trust, 70
Central Bank and Trust Company, 143
Central City Opera, 126
Central Library, **96, 185**. *See also* Denver Public Library
Central Loop, 37, **38**
Central Overland California and Pike's Peak Express, 31, **32**
Central Platte Valley, 77, 178. *See also* Platte River Valley
Central School, 39
Cervi's Newsletter, 133
Cervi's Rocky Mountain Journal, 133, 139
Cervi, Eugene, 133, **134,** 135, 139, 141, 143, 158, 170
Chaffee, Jerome, 29
Challenger Airlines, 160
Chamber of Commerce, 42

Chappell House, **80**
Chappell, Delos, 80
Charity organizations, 117–118
Chatfield Reservoir, 151
Cheeseburger, invention of, 126
Cheesman Park, **153**
Cheesman Park neighborhood, 81, 99
Cheesman Reservoir, 24, 105
Cheesman, Walter, 22, 24, 32, 41, 105, 142
Cheltenham School, 40
Cherry Creek, 1, 4, 9, 11, 15, 120
   source for drinking water, 22
Cherry Creek North shopping area, **87**
Cherry Creek Shopping Center, **84**
   original, **162**
Cheyenne Indians, 2
Children's Museum, **96,** 192
Church of the Holy Redeemer, 101
Churches, 99–101
Chutes Park, 74
Cibola Hall, 45
Cinderella City Shopping Center, 163
Citizens' Unemployment Committee, 117
Citizens Water Company, 24
City and County Building, **50,** 80, 113,
   116, 125, 86
   design and construction, 112–115
City and County of Denver, 22, 50
City Auditorium, **62,** 167
City Beautiful movement, 54–55
City Ditch, 24, **25**
City Hall building, 112
City Park, 24
City Park Golf Course, **94**
City Park neighborhood, 22
City Park zoo, 124, 168, 192
Civic Center, 54, **57, 58, 83, 85, 89, 92,**
   93, 164, 180
   plan of, **112**
   planning, 55–58
Civic Center Cultural Complex, 192
Civil War Memorial, **56**
Civil Works Administration, **119,** 120
Civilian Conservation Corps, 120–121
Clark & Company, 29
Clark, Austin M., **28**
Clark, Gruber & Company, 12, **28,** 71
Clark, Milton E., 28
Clark, William, 35
Clements neighborhood, **21**

Closing Era statue, **3**
Coal gas, 26–27, **27,** 106
Colfax Viaduct, 183
Colleges, 169–170, 193–194
Collier, D. C., 7
Colonnade of Civic Benefactors, 58, **59,**
   60, 91
Colorado Airways, 108
Colorado Central Railroad, 32
Colorado Convention Center, **150,**
   184–185
Colorado Federal Savings, 176
Colorado Historical Society, 192
Colorado National Bank, 30, **70,** 143
Colorado Ocean Journey, 179
Colorado Rockies baseball team, **88,**
   195–196
Colorado Savings and Loan, 68
Colorado School of Mines, 194
Colorado Seminary, 39
Colorado State Museum, 180
   first, 69
Colorado Symphony Orchestra, **192,** 193
Colorado Telephone Company, 26
Columbian Exposition, **3,** 52, 54
Community Chest, 117
Community College of Denver, **169,** 193
Confluence Park, 177
Congress Park, **106**
Continental Airlines, 159–160
Convention centers, 184–185
Coors brewery, 126, 146
Coors Field (baseball), **88,** 176, **178,** 179,
   183, 196, **197**
Corona School, **177**
Coronado, Francisco Vásquez de, 1
Cottrell's store, 67
Courthouse Square Project, 140
Cranmer Park, 60, **121**
Cranmer, George E., 121, 128, 157
Cranmer, Mrs. George, 80
Crawford, Dana, 152
Crawford, John, 152
Creekfront plaza, **97**
Cultural Facilities District, 192
Currigan Convention Hall, **62, 150,** 184
Currigan, Thomas, **148**
Curtis Park, **21,** 22
Curtis Theater, 77
Curtis, Samuel, 9

203

Dana, John Cotton, 42
Daniels & Fisher department store, 47, 65, **66, 149,** 176
Daniels and Fisher tower, **89, 135,** 138, **170,** 175
Daniels, Bill, 189
Daniels, William B., 65
Daniels, William Cooke, 66
Denham Theater (performing arts), 77
Denver
  as home rule city, 49
  consolidation of three towns, **10**
  formation of, 9
  founding, 7
Denver & New Orleans Railroad, 32
Denver & Rio Grande Railroad, 32, 35
Denver Art Association, 79
Denver Art Museum, **85, 116, 125,** 164, **165,** 192
  founding, 79–80
Denver Artists Club, 79
Denver Bears baseball team, **140,** 195
Denver Boot, **155**
Denver Botanic Gardens, 83, 168
Denver-Boulder Turnpike, 156–157
Denver Broncos football team, **88, 140,** 195
Denver Business Journal, 133
Denver Center for the Performing Arts, **62,** 90, **123, 191**
Denver Central Library, 192. *See also* Denver Public Library
Denver City, consolidation with Denver, **10**
Denver City and Auraria Reading Room, 40
Denver City Cable Railway Company, **36,** 37
Denver City Railway, 36
Denver City Town Company, 1, 7, 9
Denver City Water Company, 22, **23, 34**
Denver Civic Symphony, 126
Denver Civic Theater, 167
Denver Club, 142
Denver Club Building (original), 14
Denver Coliseum, 73, **147**
Denver Country Club neighborhood, 99
Denver Design Center, 65
Denver Dry Goods Company, 67, **176**
Denver Electric and Cable Company, 36
Denver Emergency Relief Committee, 118
Denver Federal Center, 129, 138, 156
Denver Gas and Electric Building, 68

Denver Gas and Electric Company, 27, 106
Denver Gas Company, 26
Denver General Hospital, 150
Denver History Museum, **16**
Denver Horse Railroad Company, 36
Denver House hotel, **31**
Denver International Airport, 30, **84,** 108, 110, **160,** 186, **187**
Denver, James, 7
Denver Landmark Preservation Commission, 153, 175
Denver Library Association, 41
Denver Metro Transit, 158
Denver Modification Center, 130
Denver Municipal Airport, **107,** 108
Denver National Bank, 68, 71, 143
Denver, Northwestern & Pacific Railroad, 35
Denver Nuggets basketball team, 179, 196
Denver Opera House, 45
Denver Ordnance Plant, 129, 138, 156
Denver Pacific Railway, 32
Denver Philharmonic Orchestra, 126
Denver Planning Commission, 115, 137, 156
Denver Planning Office, 137–138, 149, 181
Denver Post, 136, 190
Denver Public Library, 42, **43, 96,** 185
  planning, 166–167
Denver Public Schools, 169
Denver Regional Council of Governments, 149, 186
Denver square housing style, 82
Denver's Unemployed Citizens' League, 118
Denver Symphony (original), 126
Denver Symphony Orchestra, 126, 167, 193. *See also* Colorado Symphony Orchestra
Denver Tech Center, **163,** 173, **188**
Denver Theater (motion picture), 78
Denver Theater (performing arts), 45
Denver Tramway Company, 37, 38, 158
Denver U. S. National Bank, **141**
Denver Union Stockyards, 72
Denver Union Terminal Railway Company, 33
Denver Union Water Company, 24, 105
Denver United States National Bank, 71

Denver University. *See* University of Denver
Denver Urban Renewal Authority, 149–150, 173
Denver Water Board, 105, 147
Denver Water Department, 22
Denver Zephyrs baseball team, 195
Denver Zoological Gardens Foundation, 168
Department stores, 65–67
Depression of 1893, 64
Depression of 1929, 116–118
Dillon Reservoir, 148
Dora Moore School, **177**
Dougherty, M. J., 45
Downtown Denver, Incorporated, 149–181
Dravo Plaza, 175
DRCOG. *See* Denver Regional Council of Governments
Drive-in restaurants, 127
DTC. *See* Denver Tramway Corporation
Dust bowl, 116

East High School, 101, **102**
East Side High School, 39, **41**, 42
Eastlick, John, 166
Eckart, J. M., 65
Edbrooke, Frank, **13**, 19, **52**, 68, 69
Eisenhower, Dwight D., **137**
Electric service, 26
Electric streetcars, 37–38
Elephant Corral, **31**
Elitch Gardens, 46, 76–77, **92, 175,** 179
Elitch Theater, **46,** 77
Elitch, John and Mary, 46, 76
Ellsworth, Lewis C., 36
Elyria, 50
Emergency Relief and Construction Act, 118
Emerson School, **40**
Energy Center One, 172
Episcopal Methodist Church, 11
Equitable Building, **14,** 176
Ernest & Cranmer Building, 71
Evans, John (Governor), 15, **16,** 32, 39, 52
Evans, William Gray, 16

Fairmount cemetery, 25, **138**
Federal Arsenal Building, 39
Federal Emergency Relief Administration, 119–120, **124**
Federal government installations, 134
Federal Music Project, 124
Federal Reserve Bank Building, 174
Federal Theater Project, 125
Federal Writer's Project, 124
Festival of Mountain and Plain, 73–74, **93**
Fillmore Block, 12
Fillmore Plaza, **87**
Fire and Police Board, 48
Fires, 11, 33, **64, 176**
First Bank of Minneapolis, 70
First Bank System, 30
First Church of Christ, Scientists, 101
First Interstate Bank, **28,** 29
First National Bank, 29, **34,** 35, 70, 142
First National Bank of Denver, **28,** 29
First of Denver (bank), 29
Fisher, Arthur A., 59
Fisher, William E., **59**
Fisher, William M., 65
Fitzsimons Army Hospital, 130, 138
Flood of 1864, **11,** 16
Floods, 11, 16, 151
Foley's, 140
Ford Park, 74
Fort Logan, 120
Foster, A. C. Building, 68
Four Mile House, 154
410 Building, 172
Franklin School, 40
Front Range Community College, 194
Frontier Airlines, 160

Gambling, 47, 49, 51, **74**
Gano-Downs store, 67
Gas lighting, 22
Gas service, 25–27
Gates Rubber Company, 146
Gates, Charles C., 135
Gian, Bill, **97**
Glenn L. Martin Company, 145
Globe Smelter and Refining company, 13
Globeville, 22, 35, 50, 81
Gold discoveries
    Cripple Creek, 64, 73
    Little Dry Creek, 4
    in mountains, 8
    Ralston Creek, 1
Gold panning in South Platte River, 117
Goldrick, Owen J., 39

Golf, 196
Golschmann, Vladimir, 167
Good, John, **92**
Gould, George J., 33
Gove, Aaron, 39
Governor's mansion, **105**
Grace Methodist Church, 118
Grace Self-Help Co-operative, 118
Graham's Drug Store, 41
Grant-Humphreys mansion, **99**
Grant, James B., **99**
Great White Way, **77**
Greek Theater, **57,** 58, **60, 85, 91**
Gregory, John, 8
Growth, of region, 13, 33, 55, 65, 81, 134, 138, 149, 151
Gruber, E. H., 28
Guards Hall, 45
Gurley, C. D., 30

Harman, 36
Harold D. Roberts Tunnel, 148
Helen Bonfils Theater complex, 191
High Line Canal, 25, **26**
Highland, 7, 10, 20, 36, **97**
Highland Ditch, 25
Highland Park, 21
Highland Park Company, 20
Highlands, 21, 81, **97**
   annexation to Denver, 21
   town of, **10**
Highlands Ranch, **190**
Hill, Nathaniel, 13
Hilton Hotel, 140, **141**
Historic Denver, 153, 175
Historic preservation, 152–154, 175, **194**
Holladay, Ben, 31
Holladay Overland Mail & Express Company, 31
Holladay Street, 31
Homestead Act of 1862, 16
House of Lions, **154**
Housing developments, 190
Housing styles, 82
Howland, John D. "Jack", 44, **56**
Hoyt, Burnham, 102, 121, 166, 185
Hoyt, Palmer, 136
Huffman, Harry E., 78
Hughes, Gerald, 135
Humphreys, Albert E., **99**
Humphreys, Ira B., 107

Humphreys, John J., **99**
Humpty Dumpty Barrel Drive-In, 126–127

Ideal Building, 68, 176
IMAX Theater, 168
Independence Plaza, 174
Indians, treaties with, 2–3
Industrial parks, 145
Inspiration Point, 60
Insurance Exchange Building, 68
Inter-County Regional Planning Commission, 149
International Golf Tournament, 196
Interstate 25, 157
Interstate 70, 157
IntraWest Bank of Denver, 29
Inverness Business Park, 173
Irrigation, 24–25

JCRS Shopping Center, 163
Johnson, Edwin, 119
Jones Intercable, Inc., 189
Joslin's Department store, 67
Judicial/Heritage Center, 180–181

Kansas Pacific Depot, 33
Kansas Pacific Railroad, 32
Kessler, George, 59
Kittredge Building, **15,** 79, 176
Kittredge, C. H., **15**
Knight, Stephen, **61**
Kountze Brothers Bank, 30
Kountze, Charles, 30, 67
Ku Klux Klan, 108–109

Lake Archer, 22, **23**
Lake Junior High School, 102, **103**
Lake Rhoda, 25
Lakeside Amusement Park, 25, 75
Lakeside Mall, 162
Langrishe, J. S., 45
Larimer, John McMasters, 5
Larimer Square, **12, 87, 94,** 152, 176
Larimer street, survey, 9
Larimer, William H. H. (son of William H.), 5
Larimer, William H., Jr., 1, 2, 3, 5, 30
Lawrence Street Methodist Church, 12
Leadville, 32, 13
Leavenworth and Pikes Peak Express, 30–31

Libraries, 40–41, 103. *See also* Denver Public Library
Light rail, 183, **184**
Littleton Creamery-Beatrice Foods Warehouse, 65
Littleton Industrial Park, 145
Livestock Exchange Building, 72
Louisiana Purchase, 2
Lowenstein, Henry, **167**
Lowenstein Theater, **167**
Lowry Air Force Base, 129, **137,** 138
Lowry Field, 124, 128–129
Lowry Technical Training Center, 132

Machebeuf, Joseph, 39
MacMonnies, Frederick, 56
Madden, John, 173
Magafan, Ethel, 124
Magness, Bob, 189
Manhattan Beach, 46, **74,** 75
Manville Plaza, 172
Marston Lake Reservoir, 24
Martin, Glenn L. Company, 145
Martin-Marietta Corporation, 145
Masonic Building, 176
Mass transportation, 183
Mayan Theater, **78**
May D & F Department store, **50,** 66, 140, **141**
McCormick, Richard, 23
McGaa, William, 5
McNamara Dry Goods Company, 67
McNichols Arena, **118, 196**
McNichols, William H. Jr., 177, 182
Means, Rice, 108
Mechau, Frank E., 124
Mercantile Library of Denver, 42
Merchants Park, 195
Merchants Park Shopping center, 162
Methodist Episcopal Church, **7, 8,** 39
Metro Area Connection, 183
Metropolitan State College of Denver, **169,** 194
Metropolitan Theater, 45
Mile High Center, 71, **96,** 141
Mile High Stadium, 23, **140, 195**
Mining Exchange Building, 14, **70, 71**
Mints
    Clark, Gruber & Company, 12
    private, 28
    United States, 29, 71–72

Mizpah arch, **34**
Moffat, David, 15, 22, 24, 29, 32, **34,** 35, 105, 142
Moffat Depot, 35
Moffat Road, 35
Moffat Tunnel, 35–36, 122, 128
Monarch Airlines, 160
Monarch Mills, 64
Montana City, 5
Montclair, 22, 36, 44, 50, 81
Morey Junior High School, 102
Morey Mercantile Building, 65
Morley, Clarence, 108
Mount Carmel Church, 99
Mount Olivet Cemetery, 168
Mountain States Telephone and Telegraph Company, 26
Mountain View Park, 60
Mountain View Preservation ordinance, 153
Municipal Airport, 110
Municipal Art Commission, 55
Murchinson, Clinton, 142
Murchinson, John, 142
Museum of Natural History, **79, 90,** 122, 147, 192, **168, 193**
Myers, Elijah E., 18

National Recovery Act, 120
National Western Stock Show, 73, 147
Natural gas, 27, 106, 111
Neighborhood growth, 36
Neighborhoods, 15, 20, **21,** 22, 81, **157**
Neusteter, Max, 67
New Deal, 119–125
Newton, James Quigg, 136, 147, 155, 168
Nichols, Charles, 5, 7
1999 Broadway Building, 173
Ninth Street Park Historic District, 194
Norgren-Stemac, Inc., 145
North High School, 101, **102**
North Side Bank, 70
Norwest Bank, 71

Office building construction, 172–173
Office buildings, 68–69
Office parks, 163, 173
Olmstead, Frederick Law, Jr., 56
Omaha and Grant Smelter, 13
One Tabor Center, 173
On the War Trail statue, **58, 61**

207

Oriental Theater, 78
Orman, James, 49
Orpheum Theater (vaudeville), 77
Overland Park municipal golf course, 123

Palmer, William Jackson, 20, 32
Paramount Theater, 78–79
Park-and-ride facilities, **183**
Park Central, 175
Park Central Building, 70
Park Hill, 22, 36, 81
Parks, 59–60, **88**
Park system, 115
Parkways, 102
Peña, Federico, 30, 182, 186
People's Theater, 44
Petertown, **118**
Petroleum Club Building, 144
Phipps Auditorium, 122, 168
Phipps, Lawrence C., 122, 135
Pierce, Arthur E., 40–41
Pioneer monument, **54,** 56
Planter's House, 31, **32**
Platte River Valley, 151, **170, 178**
Police Building, **123**
Politics in early Denver, 47–52
Polo Club neighborhood, 99
Population, 8, 16, 20, 33, 81, 116, 134, 138, 161, 172
Poundstone amendment, 180
Poundstone, Freda J., 180
Powers, Preston, **3**
Priestman, Brian, 167
Prostitution, 47, 49, 51
Prudential Plaza, 174
Public Library of the City of Denver, 42
Public Library, The, **41**
Public Service Company of Colorado, 27, 106
Public Works Administration, 121–122

Railroads, 107
  arrival of, 13
  depots, 33–35
  establishment of, 31–36
  first service, 32
Ralston Creek, 1, 4
Ralston, Lewis, 1
Reconstruction Finance Corporation, 118
Red light districts, **51, 74**

Red Rocks amphitheater, **97, 120,** 121
Red Rocks Community College, 170, 194
Reed's Theater, 45
Regional Transportation District, 158, 181
Regis University, 194
Remington Arms Company, 129
Republic Plaza Building, 173
Richthofen, Walter von, 25, 44, 74
River Front Park, 44, 74
Robinson, Charles Mulford, 55
Rocky Flats, 139
Rocky Mountain Arsenal, 25, 129–130, 138, 160, 186
Rocky Mountain Ditch system, 25
Rocky Mountain Lake, 25
Rocky Mountain Lake Park, 60, 157
Rocky Mountain News, **189,** 190
Rocky Mountain News building, 11
Roeschlaub, Robert, **40, 48, 49,** 177
Roosevelt, Franklin D., 119
RTD. *See* Regional Transportation District
Russell, William Green, 4

St. Andrew's Episcopal Church, 101
St. Cajetan's church, 101
St. Charles Town Company, 5
St. Charles, town of, 7
St. Dominic's church, 101
St. Mary's Academy, 39
St. Patrick's Catholic Church, 99
Sakura Square, 175
Saloons, 47, **74**
Samsonite, 146
Sans Souci Gardens, 74
Schearith Israel Synagogue, **101**
School districts, 39
Schools, 39–40, 101–102, 168–169, 193
Security Life Building, **144**
Sheedy, Dennis, 13, 67
Shepherd, William C., 135
Sherman Plaza Apartment, **143**
Shoemaker, Joe, 177, 180
Shoemaker Plaza, 177
Shopping centers, 162–163
Short, Sidney, 36
Shwayder Brothers, 146
Silver prices, 52
Silver Purchase Act, 52
Sisters of Loretto, 39
Sixteenth Street, 65

Sixteenth Street Mall, **86, 89,** 181
Sixteenth Street Viaduct, **104**
Skerritt, Thomas, 15
Skyline Park, 175
Skyline Urban Renewal Project, 66, 150, 173–175
  plan, **174**
Sloan's Lake, 25, 46, 60, **74,** 75, **123**
Sloan's Lake neighborhood, 81
Smelters, 13
Smith, John, 5, 24
Smith's Ditch, **25**
Snowstorms, 182
Sopris, Indiana, 39
South Denver neighborhood, 22, 36, 81
South High School, 101
South Park & Pacific Railway, 32
South Platte River, 1, 4, 8, 9, 117, **113, 119,** 120, 177
  source for drinking water, 22
  source of irrigation, 24
South Platte River Foundation, 177
Speer Amendment, 57
Speer Boulevard, 61, **62, 182**
Speer, Kate, **113**
Speer, Robert Walter, 47–51, 54, 55–56
  boulevard planning, 59–61
  City Auditorium, 62
  park system planning, 59–61
  re-election, 57
Sports, 195–197
Spratlen-Anderson Mercantile Building, 65
Stagecoach service, 30–31, **32**
Stanley Aviation Corporation, 145
Stapleton Airfield, 108, **121,** 130, 159–160
Stapleton Airport, 147
Stapleton International Airport, 150. *See also* Denver International Airport
Stapleton, Benjamin F., 80, 108, 109, 110–111, 113, 121, 125, 132, 135, 136
State Capitol. *See* Capitol building
State Office Building, 69, **122**
Stock market crash of 1929, 115
Stockyards, 72–73
Stout, E. P., 7
Streetcars, **21,** 36–38, 158
Street lighting, 26
Streets, 17, 104, 124, **182,** 183

numbering of, 9–10
platting of, 20–21
survey of, 9, 15
Subdivisions, 22
Suburbs, 161–162
Sudler, James, 164
Sunken Gardens Park, 60
Sunset Park apartments, 175
Supreme Court, 180
Swansea, 22, 36
Symes Building, 63

Tabor Block, 13
Tabor Building, 26, 174
Tabor Grand Opera House, 13, 45
Tabor Grand Opera House building, **45**
Tabor, Horace A. W., 13, 45, 52
Tammen, Harry, 136
Tappan Building, **12**
Taste of Colorado, **73**
Taste of Colorado/Festival of Mountain and Plain, **93**
Tattered Cover Bookstore, **95**
Teikyo-Loretto Heights University, 194
Tele-Communications Incorporated, 189
Telegraph service, 26
Telephone service, 26
Temple Emanuel, 99
Temple Hoyne Buell Theater, **95,** 191
Thatcher, Joseph A., **93**
Theater (performing arts), 44–46, 77, **95,** 125, 167, 191–192
Theaters (motion picture), 78–79
Therkelsen, Peter "The Prophet", **118**
Tivoli Brewery, **92**
Tivoli Union Brewery, 126
Todd, Walter, 41
Tooley, Dale, 182
Tourism, 64, 74
Tramway Cable building, 176
Transcontinental railroad, 31
Trans-World Airlines, 160
Treaty of Fort Laramie, 2
Treaty of Fort Wise, 2–3
Trinity Methodist Episcopal Church, **48**
Trinity United Methodist Church, **48**
Trocadero Ballroom, **76**
Trolleys, 158
True, Allen, **60, 85**

Union Depot and Railroad
    Company, 33
Union Pacific railroad, 31, 35
Union Station, 14, **34,** 35, 36, 179
    (first), 33
United Airlines, 159
United Airlines Flight Center, **159**
United Bank of Denver, **96**
United States Mint, 29, **72**
United States National Bank, 70, 71
University Building, **68**
University Hall, **49**
University of Colorado at Denver, 169, 193
University of Denver, 39, **49,** 194
Unsinkable Molly Brown, **154**
U. S. National Bank Building, 71, 140
Utility services, 26–27, 63, 105–106

Valley Highway, **121, 156,** 157
Valverde, 50
Viaducts, 183
Voorhies, John H. P., **59**
Voorhies Memorial, 58, **59,** 63

Wagon trains, **31**
Wahlberg, Edgar M., 118
Walhalla Hall, 45
Walker's Castle, **44**
Walker, John Brisben, **44**
Wallace, George, 163
Washington Park, 24, 60, **88**
Washington Park neighborhood, 81

Water companies, 24
Water supply, 24–25, 122, 147–148
    early sources for, 22–24
Webb and Knapp, Inc., 132, 139
Wells Fargo Express, **12**
Western Air Express, 108
Western Airlines, 108
Western Federal Savings Building, 144
Western Livestock Show, 73
Western Union Company, 26
West High School, 101
West Side Pump Station, **23**
Westword, 190
Willis Case municipal golf course, **94,** 123
Willison, Robert, 62
Winter Park Ski area, 128
Wolcott, Henry, 142
Wolff, Hiram, 25
Woodbury branch library, 103
Woodbury, Roger W., 42, **103**
Works Progress Administration,
    123, **125**
World War II, 128–132
World Youth Day, 100
Writer's Square, **84**

Zang Mansion, **82**
Zang, Adolph, **82**
Zang, Philip, **82**
Zeckendorf, William, 132, 139–140
Zietz, Henry H., **197**
Zoo, 192. *See also* City park zoo